PLANETS, STARS, AND GALAXIES

PHYSICS IN ACTION

PLANETS, STARS, AND GALAXIES

Gordon Ritter

Series Editor
David G. Haase

CHELSEA HOUSE
PUBLISHERS
An imprint of Infobase Publishing

PLANETS, STARS, AND GALAXIES

Chelsea House
An imprint of Infobase Publishing
132 West 31st Street
New York, NY 10001

Library of Congress Cataloging-in-Publication Data

Ritter, Gordon.
  Planets, stars, and galaxies / Gordon Ritter.
      p. cm. — (Physics in action)
  Includes bibliographical references and index.
  ISBN-13: 978-0-7910-8933-0 (hardcover)
  ISBN-10: 0-7910-8933-9 (hardcover)
  1. Astrophysics. 2. Cosmology. I. Title.
  QB461.R48 2007
  523.1—dc22
                                          2007015334

Chelsea House books are available at special discounts when purchased in bulk quantities for businesses, associations, institutions, or sales promotions. Please call our Special Sales Department in New York at (212) 967–8800 or (800) 322–8755.

You can find Chelsea House on the World Wide Web at http://www.chelseahouse.com

Text design by James Scotto-Lavino
Cover design by Ben Peterson

Printed in the United States of America

Bang NMSG 10 9 8 7 6 5 4 3

This book is printed on acid-free paper.

All links and Web addresses were checked and verified to be correct at the time of publication. Because of the dynamic nature of the Web, some addresses and links may have changed since publication and may no longer be valid.

CONTENTS

120249

Introduction

THE ATTEMPT TO UNDERSTAND THE UNIVERSE'S SEEMINGLY infinite mysteries is a great adventure that can surely provide one with merriment, frustration, joy, sadness, and continual wonder and amazement throughout all of one's life. The fundamental principles governing the operation of the universe and the way in which it forms structure always seem just beyond our grasp, and during every age of human history that supported the practice of science, it was believed that the state of knowledge was "mostly complete" with a few "loose ends" to be tied up. Often, however, a new cataclysmic discovery would completely change our conception of the natural world, and such new knowledge is always waiting patiently, just around the corner, to be uncovered.

The intended audience for this book includes anyone who has ever been outside at night and stopped to wonder about the night sky, with questions such as: How large is the universe? Is it infinite or finite? What is its structure? What kinds of matter and energy does the universe contain and what are the physical laws that govern their motion and interactions? How did the universe begin and what is its ultimate fate? This section is an invitation to each reader of this book. You are invited to ask these questions and to tirelessly seek their answers. In so doing, you will join a group of individuals who were not content merely to live in the universe, but who wanted to know precisely *where* they live, *what* is possible in this place, and *how* they came to be there. This book may help you to learn some of the tools you will need on your journey, including some mathematics, and some physical intuition. If one person is inspired by this book to become a physicist, it will be a tremendous success.

We end this invitation with a biographical snippet from the life of one of the twentieth century's greatest physicists. Lise Meitner (1878–1968) was born in Vienna, Austria, the third of eight children of a Viennese Jewish family (*Figure 1.0*). Her father was a lawyer. Meitner was initially encumbered by restrictions that banned women from studying at institutions of higher education, but these were lifted in time for her to enter the University of Vienna in 1901, where she received her doctorate in physics in 1905 under Ludwig Boltzmann. (Boltzmann was one of the founders of modern thermodynamics.) Upon Boltzmann's death in 1907, Meitner moved to Berlin, where she studied with Max Planck (the discoverer of quantum theory whose work on blackbody radiation will be discussed later in this book) and with the chemist Otto Hahn. Despite obstacles such as the interruption of World War I, in which she served as a front-line nurse, Meitner became a full professor and the head of her own section at the Kaiser-Wilhelm Institute in Berlin. In 1926 at the University of Berlin, Meitner became the first woman in Germany to achieve the rank of full professor in any field of study. Because of her Jewish background, in 1938 Meitner fled from Germany to Stockholm, Sweden. This was a perilous and difficult journey; during the crossing from Germany into the Netherlands, she was forced to abandon all of her possessions.

Meitner made many fundamental contributions to physics despite the considerable difficulties she faced. One that stands out is her work with her nephew Otto Frisch that explained nuclear fission using Bohr's "liquid drop" model of the nucleus. This was an immediate precursor to the Manhattan Project and to the development of nuclear energy.

In a 1964 essay titled "Looking Back," Meitner wrote:

Figure 1.0 *Lise Meitner was an Austrian physicist who made significant contributions to our understanding of radioactivity and nuclear physics.*

I believe all young people think about how they would like their lives to develop; when I did so, I always arrived at the conclusion that life need not be easy, provided only that it is not empty. That life has not always been easy—the First and Second World Wars and their consequences saw to that—while for the fact that it has indeed been full, I have to thank the wonderful developments of physics during my lifetime and the great and lovable personalities with whom my work in physics brought me contact.

It is hoped that your association with physics also brings you into contact with such "great and lovable personalities" as those whom Meitner describes!

The subject of this book—the structure of the universe and how the Earth fits into it—is vast. There were many possible routes one could take in a book about this topic. The author has chosen a route that leads the reader on a whirlwind tour of a few of the great scientists of antiquity, their lives, and their discoveries. Any book promising to describe the Earth's relationship with the rest of the universe must at least contain a discussion of Newton's physics and Einstein's relativity. In order to understand these concepts, it is important to know some basic ideas from calculus. Only a small amount of prerequisite mathematical training is needed in order to begin the book, and we will develop the rest of what is needed as we go along. Armed with these tools, the later chapters introduce the reader to astronomy and cosmology, just barely scratching the surface of these exciting fields. The reader should view this book not as a complete reference book for astronomy, cosmology, and classical physics, but rather as a seedling that could grow in almost any direction.

The basic information one needs to begin a life in physics is here. To make the most of it, one should think critically about what you read both in texts and in the popular press; to be sure, it's not the whole story. Look up the references, then look at the references you find there, and pursue relentlessly the questions that stand out to you.

CHAPTER 1

The Universe
(and Welcome to It!)

OUR SOLAR SYSTEM IS KNOWN TO CONTAIN THE SUN; THE eight official planets (in order of increasing distance from the Sun: Mercury, Venus, Earth, Mars, Jupiter, Saturn, Uranus, and Neptune), at least three "dwarf planets" (Pluto is now classified as a dwarf planet), more than 130 satellites of the planets, and a large number of comets, asteroids, and floating debris. There are probably also many more planetary satellites waiting to be discovered, and some of the known planetary satellites (or "moons") are themselves comparable in size to small planets. A large asteroid belt lies between the orbits of Mars and Jupiter. An examination of a diagram of the planets reflecting their relative sizes may provoke the reaction that Earth is very tiny compared to Uranus and Neptune, which are themselves tiny compared to Jupiter and Saturn, and all are tiny when compared to the Sun (*Figure 1.1*). The four large planets make up about 99% of the mass known to orbit the Sun.

Beyond Neptune lies the "Kuiper belt," a large shell of objects about 30,000 to 50,000 times farther from the Sun than Earth.

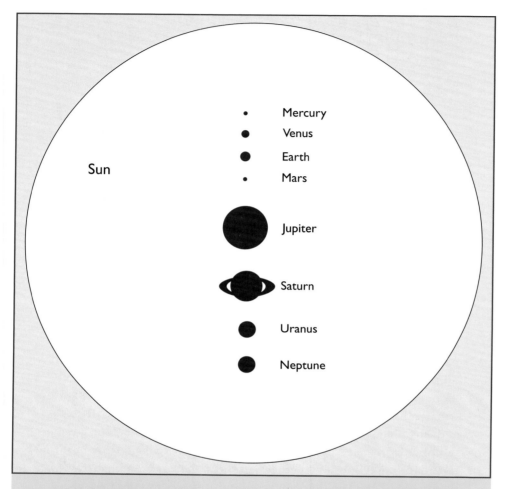

Figure 1.1 *Relative sizes of the planets and the Sun. Note that the distances to the Sun are not to scale.*

Gerard Kuiper suggested in 1951 that comet-like debris left over from the formation of the solar system should be just beyond Neptune. Moreover, Kuiper argued convincingly that it would be most unusual *not* to find a continuum of particles beyond the part of the solar system occupied by the large planets. The reason for this is that, since the large objects of the solar system were formed by the condensation of smaller particles, it is very unlikely for such a process of formation to leave a discrete "edge" at its boundary. Some very remote and surprising Kuiper belt objects have been discovered using the Hubble Space Telescope, including, for instance, an "ice planet" half the size of Pluto!

All of the planets orbit the Sun, following elliptical paths (the precise definition of an ellipse will come later), just as Newtonian physics would predict. Each planet has its own orbital period, which is the time it takes to make one revolution around the Sun. For the Earth, this period is approximately 365 days, or one Earth-year. Each planet's elliptical orbit lies in a certain plane in three-dimensional space, and for our solar system, the planes for different planets are, in a first approximation, aligned. In a rough, approximate sense, one can speak of "the plane of the solar system."

It is important to stress that our modern level of knowledge of the solar system is built upon millennia of advances both in fundamental theoretical physics and in the science of observation, with one type of advance building upon the others. The Hubble Space Telescope gives us precise knowledge of distant parts of the universe that could never have been derived through purely theoretical investigations, but without many important theoretical advances (such as Newtonian mechanics, general relativity, and electromagnetism), such a telescope could never have been built and put into practice. In the next section we will give an incomplete history of some of the most important scientific breakthroughs that enabled our current, fairly detailed understanding of the solar system to evolve into its present form.

PHYSICS HISTORY, LEGEND, AND FOLKLORE

This section is dedicated to a brief, informal history of the attempts by our predecessors to understand the motions of planets, stars, and galaxies, which ultimately culminated in Isaac Newton's invention of calculus and of the associated theory of physics now known as Newtonian mechanics. Newton's mechanics included the first modern concept of "force" and the rules by which forces influence the motion of bodies. We will give a brief, modernized account of Newton's ideas in Chapter 2. Newton achieved the first successful mathematical explanation of planetary motion; while his description of planetary physics is now known to be only approximately correct, even by modern standards, the approximation is quite good. Tiny corrections to Newton's mechanics, which can be properly explained by Einstein's general theory of relativity, give a description of the mechanics of our solar system that is accurate to many decimal places and has passed all experimental tests thus far.

Claudius Ptolemy, an Egyptian living in Alexandria around A.D. 150, wrote a seminal work on astronomy now called the *Almagest*. Its original title was something like *The Mathematical Compilation*, while the name *Almagest* derives from an Arabic translation of the title. The *Almagest* consists of 13 books containing compilations of measurements of our solar system, with accompanying mathematical theories to explain them. These "theories" ultimately proved to be of little use, because they are not explanations of fundamental physical processes, and hence we should not even expect them to lead to a general theory of mechanics. Instead, they are guesses about possible mathematical descriptions for the planets' motions, based on study of observational data.

One of the fundamental flaws in Ptolemy's "theory" is that it's based on the Earth-centered (or "geocentric") concept of Aristotle. This view of the world contends that the Earth is fixed, while other objects (such as the Sun, Moon, stars, and planets) rotate around this fixed center. Modern physicists would agree that the statement "the Earth is fixed" has no intrinsic meaning, because it does not provide the answer to the question: "Fixed with respect to what?" Based on such (rather illogical) premises, Ptolemy predicted the positions of the Sun, Moon, and planets using **epicycles**, the curves traced out by a point on a circle that rolls along another circle (*Figure 1.2*). Many of these predictions do not match the data well, because the correct equations of motion are not those of an epicycle.

Modern reasoning would point out that even on Earth on a dark night, a brighter torch viewed at a greater distance may appear to be the same brightness as a smaller, nearer torch. Thus, simply observing the brightness of an object in the night sky can never suffice to determine its distance from us. The determination of distance in astronomy can be very difficult, for precisely this reason, and it generally must involve at least two measurements made from different points on the Earth's orbit.

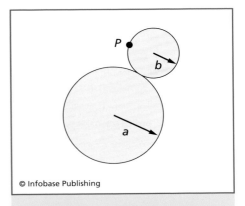

© Infobase Publishing

Figure 1.2 *Ptolemy used epicycles, the curves traced out by a point on a circle that rolls along another circle, to predict the positions of the Sun, Moon, and planets.*

Though he lived long before Ptolemy, Aristarchus (310–230 B.C.) had a remarkably modern picture of astronomy. Although some of Aristarchus's most important writings were lost, it is generally believed that he proposed a heliocentric (or sun-centered) model 1,700 years before Copernicus, one of the central figures in astronomy who we will introduce shortly. Archimedes writes in *The Sand Reckoner*:

> . . . the "universe" is the name given by most astronomers to the sphere the centre of which is the centre of the Earth, while its radius is equal to the straight line between the centre of the Sun and the centre of the Earth. This is the common account as you have heard from astronomers. But Aristarchus has brought out a book consisting of certain hypotheses, wherein it appears, as a consequence of the assumptions made, that the universe is many times greater than the 'universe' just mentioned. His hypotheses are that the fixed

stars and the Sun remain unmoved, that the Earth revolves
about the Sun on the circumference of a circle, the Sun lying
in the middle of the orbit, and that the sphere of fixed stars,
situated about the same centre as the Sun, is so great that the
circle in which he supposes the Earth to revolve bears such a
proportion to the distance of the fixed stars as the center of
the sphere bears to its surface.

Perhaps due to the clarity of exposition and apparent mathematical rigor of Ptolemy's *Almagest*, its flawed theories (including the
geocentric model) would be generally accepted for at least 1,500
years after its publication.

Nicolaus Copernicus (1473–1543) is often credited with the
beginning of modern astronomy (*Figure 1.3*). He was born in Poland, and studied mathematics and optics at Krakow University.
After returning to Poland from several years' study of church
law in Bologna, Italy, Copernicus was appointed as a priest in
the cathedral of Frauenburg (now known as Frombork, in north-
ern Poland), where the rest of his life was sheltered and devoted
to scholarship.

Although astronomy gradually grew to be his primary interest, Copernicus was also a painter and a translator of poetry. He
made celestial observations from a turret situated on the defensive
wall around the cathedral of Frauenburg. Copernicus' celestial
observations were made with the naked eye, since telescopes had
not yet been invented. In 1530, Copernicus completed his mas-
terpiece, *De Revolutionibus*, which asserted that the Earth spins
once every 24 hours about an internal axis, while at the same time
making a complete trip around the Sun once every 365 days. This
idea was audacious and flew in the face of all of the commonly accepted wisdom of the time.

Copernicus's publisher apparently added a statement that
the model was only a mathematical device to calculate planetary
positions that did not reflect reality. This assertion was unfair
to Copernicus, because his mathematical devices did correctly
reflect certain aspects of reality. Although Copernicus fell short

Figure 1.3 *Nicolaus Copernicus (1473–1543) was the astronomer who formulated the first heliocentric (sun-centered) theory of the solar system, in which the Earth spins once every 24 hours about an internal axis, while at the same time making a complete trip around the Sun once every 365 days.*

String Theory

Some wonder whether the branch of theoretical physics known as string theory should be described as only a mathematical device. The theory, which assumes the existence of tiny strings, much smaller even than protons or quarks, gave rise to a mathematical model for calculation of short-distance effects of gravitation, such as Stephen Hawking's celebrated theory that black holes, if not gaining mass from outside, will lose mass and eventually evaporate. The strings themselves cannot be seen directly, but the mathematical model arising from string theory seems compelling for many purposes.

of achieving a general theory of mechanics that could be applied to billiard balls as well as to planets and that might explain *why* the Earth rotates about the Sun, his qualitative picture of the Earth's rotation about its own axis and about the Sun was right on the mark.

Copernicus died peacefully in 1543 and was never to know the upheaval that his work had caused within the Catholic Church. Other founders of modern astronomy, on the other hand, did not fare as well.

Giordano Bruno (1548–1600), unlike Copernicus' publisher, gladly adopted Copernicus's heliocentric model as the truth. Born near Naples, Italy, the son of Giovanni Bruno, a soldier, and Fraulissa Savolino, Bruno took the name Giordano upon entering the Dominican order. From 1583 to 1585, Bruno lived at the house of the French ambassador in London. During this period he wrote *Cena de le Ceneri* ("The Ash Wednesday Supper") and *De l'Infinito Universo e Mondi* ("On the Infinite Universe and Worlds"), both published in 1584. In *Cena de le Ceneri*, Bruno defended the heliocentric theory of Copernicus. Though Bruno's understanding of the technical details of astronomy was confused on several points, his predictions for the overall structure of space and for the matter that it contains were much closer to our modern understanding than any other prevailing theory of the time. In Copernicus's model, the stars were believed to be part of a finite sphere that encased the solar system. In *De l'Infinito Universo e Mondi*, Bruno hypothesized that they were actually distant suns scattered throughout a universe infinite in size, and that around these suns circled planets similar to those in our solar system. Bruno also predicted the existence of additional planets orbiting the Sun beyond the orbit of Saturn (the most distant planet known at the time), which, he hypothesized, were too distant to be seen. We now know, of course, that Uranus and Neptune fit Bruno's description.

Bruno was a philosopher whose writings sometimes diverge into medieval mysticism and magic. For example, Bruno's belief that the Earth circled the Sun seems to have been connected with a conception that the Earth may be a living creature in and of itself. Similarly, Bruno's belief in an infinite universe, filled with innumerable planets circling other stars, came not through the scientific method, but from religious mysticism.

It is also clear from Bruno's writing that he had the correct conception that these planets could not be seen because they were fainter (or less luminous) than their stars. To illustrate his point, he used a naval analogy. Suppose that we see a large ship docked at a nearby harbor, and it is surrounded by small boats. It is then a very reasonable supposition that, if we then see a large ship in the distance, said Bruno, it should also be surrounded by small boats, even though we will not be able to see them. Thus Bruno illustrated that the near and the far obey the same laws of physics. "We are a celestial body for the Moon and for every other celestial body," wrote Bruno, "and we are the firmament just as much as they are for us." He thus contradicted Aristotle, who had held that the Earth, flawed and imperfect, was separate from the heavens, which were perfect and which never change—the latter being a more appealing idea to the Church! For these views, Bruno was arrested and tried by the Inquisition, an organization within the Catholic Church that was responsible for the elimination of heretics, those who held opinions contrary to those of the Church. He was ultimately found guilty of eight heresies and burned at the stake.

For precisely the reason Bruno pointed out—their low intrinsic tendency to produce light—it follows that distant planets are very difficult to detect. Only in the 1990s, four centuries after Bruno's death, did astronomers finally succeed in detecting genuine planets around other stars, thus confirming Bruno's prediction.

In May 1609, Galileo Galilei (1564–1642), by then a professor at the University of Padua, Italy, received a letter from Paolo Sarpi telling him about a man in Holland who had constructed a "spyglass" that had been displayed in Venice (*Figure 1.4*). From these and other reports, Galileo crafted a series of telescopes whose optical performance was much better than that of the Dutch spyglass. His first telescope was made from available lenses and gave a magnification of about four times. Eventually, Galileo learned how to grind and polish his own lenses, and by August 1609 he was able to make a telescope with a magnification similar to a set of inexpensive modern binoculars.

In December 1609 and January 1610, Galileo made an incredible number of revolutionary astronomical discoveries using his newly invented telescope. He described these discoveries in a short book called *Starry Messenger (Siderius Nuncius)*, published in Venice in May 1610. This work, in which Galileo reported that there were mountains on the Moon, that the Milky Way was made up of tiny stars, and that four small bodies orbited Jupiter, caused a sensation.

In 1616, Galileo wrote a letter to the Grand Duchess Christina of Lorraine to argue in favor of a nonliteral interpretation of Holy Scripture when the literal interpretation would contradict facts about the physical world proved by mathematical science. This letter also confirmed Galileo's view of the Copernican theory. In it, he wrote that he believed that the Earth rotates on itself and moves around the Sun, refuting both Ptolemy's and Aristotle's arguments.

Galileo was examined by the Church in 1633, and was eventually forced, under the threat of torture and death, to renounce all belief in Copernican theories. Galileo was thereafter sentenced to imprisonment (this became a mild sort of imprisonment, which might today be called "house arrest," partially due to Galileo's failing health) for the remainder of his days. In addition to the invention of the telescope, and the corresponding profound impact it had upon astronomy (and, indeed, on all of physics), Galileo correctly worked out various aspects of the motion of bodies under the influence of gravitation. In particular, he gave correct descriptions of the acceleration of bodies along inclined planes and in freefall, which would be later confirmed by Newtonian mechanics. This shows Galileo's versatility: he devised experiments, invented and built the experimental apparatus, and developed theories to explain the outcome of those experiments.

Figure 1.4 *The achievements of Galileo Galilei (1564–1642) include the invention of the telescope and a multitude of astronomical discoveries.*

THEORY VERSUS FACT

In the following chapters, we will describe some very exciting aspects of physics; some of these are exciting precisely because they flagrantly contradict some of a person's intuition about everyday physics. Einstein's relativity is perhaps the best-known example. Einstein taught us that there is no good (i.e. unambiguous) definition of concepts that we take for granted, such as the ability to tell whether or not two events happened at the same time; this is called the **relativity of simultaneity.** The counterintuitive statements of quantum theory are still more bizarre; there is an extremely small (but non-zero!) probability that a bullet could pass directly through a brick wall without damaging the wall.

Physics at high velocities and small distances does not behave at all like the physics at low energy and normal distances, so these statements may shock us when we first hear them. Because of these discrepancies, people who work in fields other than science often have the misconception that some of these statements are "wild, imaginative theories" that, while interesting mathematically, have little or no relation to real-world physics. In fact, the seemingly counter-intuitive assertions of quantum mechanics and relativity theory are verified over and over again in laboratories and in electronic devices (such as cellular phones and GPS devices) all over the world.

There are elements of modern physics that are more speculative. For example, there is controversy about the number of dimensions of space in our universe. No one disputes that at length scales comparable to those of everyday life, and with traditional measuring devices (in particular, the five senses), it appears that there are three dimensions of space, $d = 3$. But is this exactly true, or is it an approximation? Is it possible that $d = 3 + k$, and that the additional k dimensions remain hidden to all but the most sensitive measurements? No one knows the answer to this question with certainty, but what we can say with certainty is that no experiment that has so far been done is capable of ruling out the possibility that the extra dimensions exist.

The theory of these extra dimensions is, then, necessarily somewhat speculative, while relativity and quantum mechanics have been tested in many thousands or millions of experiments of various kinds, and are on solid ground. For the reader who is not a professional physicist, how is it possible to tell whether the author is describing a theory that has been well-tested and is on firm experimental ground or one that is a creative idea that is yet to be ruled out, but also not known to be true?

For the convenience of the reader who may be bewildered at the possibility of not knowing which theory to trust, in this book I have chosen to treat only topics that are solidly grounded in experiment. While the debate may continue about how to properly interpret quantum mechanics, to dispute that quantum theory is at least a good approximate description of atomic physics (for instance) would be tantamount to disbelieving the hard data that comes out of thousands of experiments. Direct disbelief of something that has been well understood by one's predecessors is generally counterproductive to the progress of science. This is not to say these theories could not be extended or improved; in fact, it is essential for the continued progress of humanity that we continue to refine and improve our understanding of nature.

The theories described in this book are almost always of the well-established and well-tested type. The one possible exception is the discussion of the structure of the universe in Chapter 6. Since we can't directly observe the universe at very early times, many of the conclusions assume that information can be obtained by observing trends that exist now, and extrapolating the trend backward in time. Also in cosmology, the actual values of certain of the physical parameters, such as the Hubble parameter, have proven notoriously difficult to measure (but even in those cases, measurements constrain the parameter to lie in a certain range, and the range continuously shrinks as the measuring process improves). Therefore, some of my statements about the early universe are subject to argument; still, I wish to reassure the reader that the viewpoint I have endeavored to explain is that of the majority of the experts in the field.

CHAPTER 2

The Mathematics of Motion

Philosophy is written in this grand book—I mean the universe—which stands open to our gaze, but it cannot be understood unless one first learns to comprehend the language and interpret the characters in which it is written. It is written in the language of mathematics, and its characters are triangles, circles, and other geometrical figures, without which it is humanly impossible to understand a single word of it; without these, one is wandering about in a dark labyrinth. (Galileo, *The Assayer*)

GRAVITY IS EXPERIENCED BY THE EVERYDAY OBSERVER because it changes the motion of objects. If you jump up from the surface of the Earth with some initial velocity, say, 1 meter/second, then before you get very far, gravity will quickly adjust your velocity to be back towards the surface of the Earth, and you will be pulled back to the ground. Therefore, gravity is something that changes velocities. The strength of gravity is measured by how much it can change the velocity of an object. Before we can obtain a quantitative understanding of gravity, we must develop one simple mathematical tool that shows us how to calculate the change in the velocity of a moving body. This simple mathematical tool, the slope of a curve, turns out to be fundamental in every branch of science. If you have never calculated the slope of a curve before, it's important and worthwhile to take enough time to carefully check every step of the calculations in this chapter. The only mathematical prerequisite for reading this chapter is a familiarity with algebra and the concept of a function.

A CONCRETE EXAMPLE

Let's begin with a concrete example. Consider the function $f(t) = t^2$, whose graph is a parabola (*Figure 2.1*). Our problem is to calculate the slope of the line through the two points $(1, 1)$ and $(1 + h, 1 + 2h + h^2)$. Let's agree to call this line ℓ_h. Both points lie on the graph of $f(t)$ for any real number h, so the line ℓ_h always crosses the graph in two points unless $h = 0$, in which case it crosses in one

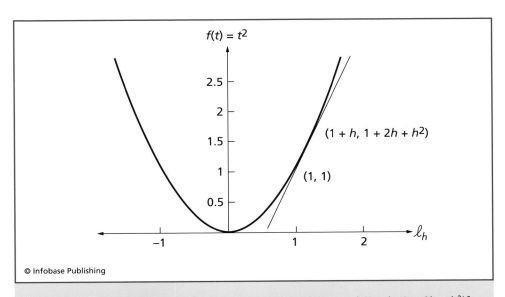

Figure 2.1 *The parabola y = t², with the two points [(1,1) and (1 + h, 1 + 2h + h²)] labeled.*

point. Recall that **slope** is defined for a line $y = mx + b$ to be the number m, and that given two points (x_1, y_1) and (x_2, y_2) on this line, we can calculate m by the formula

$$m = \frac{y_2 - y_1}{x_2 - x_1}$$

To get the slope of ℓ_h, all we have to do is plug in and calculate:

$$m = \frac{1 + 2h + h^2 - 1}{1 + h - 1} \tag{2.1}$$

This is the answer, but some additional algebraic simplification will be worthwhile. Note the cancellation:

$$m = \frac{1 + 2h + h^2 - 1}{1 + h - 1} = \frac{2h + h^2}{h} = \frac{(2 + h)h}{h} = 2 + h \tag{2.2}$$

Taking $h = 0$ seems to make no sense: how could we calculate a unique slope for the line through only one point? Aren't there many lines through one point, all with different slopes? On the other hand, Equation 2.2 tells us unambiguously that at $h = 0$, the answer is $m = 2$.

The important point is that substituting $h = 0$ into Equation 2.1 gives 0/0, which looks like nonsense. To say $a/b = k$ just means $a = bk$, so $0/0 = k$ would mean that $0 = 0k$, but this is satisfied for any number k that you can imagine! It is much more instructive to look at the expression

$$m = \frac{(2 + h)h}{h}$$

which appeared in Equation 2.2. Keep $h > 0$, but continue to lower h as much as possible towards zero without actually reaching zero. During the whole process, the small h's in the numerator and denominator still cancel. All the while, m is getting closer and closer to the value $m = 2$.

This situation occurs so often in mathematics that it has been given a special name: we say that the limit as $h \to 0$ of m equals 2.

The notation for this is $\lim_{h \to 0} m = 2$. Geometrically, it's clear that our line ℓ_h for $h = 0$ becomes a **tangent line**, which is a line that crosses the curve in exactly one point.

There's nothing particularly special about the point (1, 1) as far as the parabola is concerned. We could have just as easily calculated the slope at some general point (t, t^2) for some real number t by the same method. In Equation 2.2 we would have found

$$m = \frac{t^2 + 2ht + h^2 - t^2}{t + h - t} = \frac{2th + h^2}{h} = \frac{(2t + h)h}{h} = 2t + h \qquad (2.3)$$

We can now see that m depends on both t and h; it is a function of two variables, so perhaps $m(t, h)$ would have been a better notation, and we will in fact use this later. As h approaches zero, m approaches $2t$.

PHYSICAL UNITS

Of fundamental importance in physics is the distance an object has traveled as a function of time. In its present form, it is impossible that $f(t) = t^2$ could represent a distance, because t is a time (say) measured in hours. Then $f(t) = t^2$ has units of hr^2, where "hr" is an abbreviation for "hour." The term "hour squared," however, is a rather useless unit. This situation can be remedied by introducing a constant a with units of km/hr^2, and redefining $f(t) = at^2$. Here, "km" denotes the kilometer, a distance measure defined in terms of the speed of light, and equal to about 0.62 miles. With this redefinition, clearly $f(t)$ is measured in kilometers.

What about the slope? Repeating the calculation of (2.3) for this case and taking h to zero gives

$$m = 2at$$

for $f(t) = at^2$. Therefore m has units of

$$\frac{km}{hr^2} hr = \frac{km}{hr}$$

or, in words, kilometers per hour. We could also measure m in miles per hour by multiplying all speeds by 0.62. In either case, m has the familiar units of speed, as measured on the dashboard of a car.

SLOPE AND RATE OF CHANGE

Now consider a completely general function, $f = f(t)$, which depends on an independent variable t, which we will think of as time. We will use the Greek letter delta (δ), to mean "change in," which saves a lot of writing. Consider a very small change in time; the concretely minded reader may think that $\delta t \approx 0.0001$ sec throughout this discussion, although the arguments are general. Note that above, the variable h played the role of a change in time, so we will make the replacement $h = \delta t$ in what follows.

From the initial time t to the final time $t + \delta t$, this function has changed by an amount

$$\delta f = f(t + \delta t) - f(t)$$

As we will consider time intervals of various lengths, of greater interest is the total change in f per unit time, or **average rate of change,** which is obtained by dividing the previous expression by the length of the time interval,

$$\frac{\delta f}{\delta t} = \frac{f(t + \delta t) - f(t)}{\delta t} \tag{2.4}$$

Change per unit time is also called the rate of change. By analogy with the calculation of Equation 2.2, Equation 2.4 also arises if we calculate the slope of the line through the two points $(t, f(t))$ and $(t + \delta t, f(t + \delta t))$, both of which lie on the graph of the function $f(t)$. A line that intersects a curve in exactly two points is called a **secant line.** We have observed that Equation 2.4 is the slope of the secant line through the two indicated points.

To know what is going on at a particular instant corresponds to taking a very short time interval around that instant, so δt

approaches zero. It was absolutely crucial in Equation 2.3 that the numerator $2th + h^2$ can be *factored*, giving $(2t + h)h$. This allowed the cancellation of the extra h in the numerator with the h in the denominator.

Suppose the function $f(t)$ has the property that δf, as defined above, can have a δt factored out:

$$\delta f = f(t + \delta t) - f(t) = \delta t\, m(t, \delta t)$$

where $m(t, \delta t)$ is some function of two variables. Plugging into the above, we find

$$\frac{\delta f}{\delta t} = \frac{f(t + \delta t) - f(t)}{\delta t} = m(t, \delta t)$$

Assuming that m is defined everywhere, we may take δt to be zero exactly, and conclude that the instantaneous rate of change at time t is $m(t, 0)$. As discussed previously, this is also the slope of the tangent line to the curve at $(t, f(t))$. In Equation 2.4, we could not have taken δt to be zero exactly, because δt appears in the denominator.

There are two notations used all over the world for $m(t, 0)$. One is $f'(t)$, and the other is df/dt. We now have three notations for the same thing:

$$\frac{df}{dt} = f'(t) = m(t, 0) \qquad (2.5)$$

and three is one too many. We will henceforth abandon the (cumbersome) $m(t, 0)$ notation, and use df/dt and $f'(t)$ interchangeably. Of the remaining two notations, each has its advantages and disadvantages. The advantage of the df/dt notation is that it emphasizes this function's beginnings as a limit, as $\delta t \to 0$, of the finite quotient (Equation 2.4), and indeed, there are certain cases in which df/dt behaves literally as if it were a fraction. One then imagines df and dt as sides of an infinitely small triangle, which gives useful intuition. In particular, we will encounter these infinitesimal triangles later on, when we study the concept of arc length in the type of curved spacetime used by Einstein in his theory of relativity, and the intuition of df/dt as a quotient of very small pieces will be very useful. On the other hand, the notation $f'(t)$ makes it very straightforward to write functional relationships, like the chain rule, which we will encounter later in this chapter.

A WONDERFUL MATHEMATICAL TOOL

The operation that takes a function f and returns a new function f' representing the rate of change of the old function is a wonderful mathematical tool known as the **derivative**. This concept is also relevant in biology: if $f'(t)$ represents the number of bacteria in a culture dish at time t, then $f'(t)$ is the rate at which the bacteria reproduce themselves. As long as there is enough space and resources in the dish, then (for bacteria) $f'(t)$ will be approximately proportional to $f'(t)$. In fact, this determines which function $f'(t)$ is required to be, up to a constant!

Before continuing, it is important to give a few properties of our wonderful mathematical tool. For $n > 2$, this calculation may be performed by the binomial theorem, a general result that expresses $(x + y)^n$ in terms of powers of x and y. This can even be made to work for fractional n, although more care is necessary. One finds for all n the result

$$\frac{d}{dt}t^n = nt^{n-1} \qquad (2.6)$$

For $n = 2$, this reproduces the result of the first calculation from this chapter. This is called the **power rule**.

A crucial property of the derivative is linearity, which means that

$$\frac{d}{dt}(f + ch) = \frac{d}{dt}f + c\frac{d}{dt}h$$

where f, h are any two functions whose derivatives exist, and c is any constant. There are also convenient rules for calculating derivatives of more complicated functions, if you know how to do it for simple functions. We mention the **product rule**, the rule for finding the derivative of a product function:

$$(fg)' = f'g + fg' \qquad (2.7)$$

and the **chain rule**, the rule for finding the derivative of a composed function:

$$\frac{d}{dt} f(g(t)) = f'(g(t))\, g'(t). \qquad (2.8)$$

You might say that Equation 2.7 looks great for calculating the derivative of a product; but what about quotients? What is $(f/g)'$? To answer this, note that

$$\frac{f}{g} = f\, g^{-1}$$

where $g^{-1} = 1/g$ by definition (the -1 exponent does not mean the inverse function).

We could apply the product rule if only we knew $\frac{d}{dt}(g^{-1})$. The latter, however, is calculated by the chain rule and the power rule, together! Let's do this explicitly, to solidify our understanding. The power rule (Equation 2.6) for $n = -1$ gives us $\frac{d}{dt}(t^{-1}) = -t^{-2}$. Then Equation 2.8 tells us that

$$\frac{d}{dt}(g^{-1}) = -g^{-2}\, g' = \frac{-g'}{g^2}.$$

The product rule now gives

$$\frac{d}{dt}\frac{f}{g} = \frac{d}{dt}(f\, g^{-1}) = f\frac{d}{dt}(g^{-1}) + \frac{df}{dt} g^{-1} = \frac{-f g'}{g^2} + \frac{f'}{g} = \frac{f'g - f g'}{g^2}.$$

This formula is called the **quotient rule**. It follows from the other rules.

INSTANTANEOUS RATE OF CHANGE

Instantaneous rate of change is one of the most fundamental concepts in physics. The rate of change of the position of an object is called the **velocity**. Normally, one speaks of velocity in a certain direction, but when there is only one direction, the velocity is described by a single number called the **speed** and corresponds to the reading on a car's speedometer.

Let t denote the number of seconds from the time that one has thrown a baseball straight up from the Earth's surface. Let $x(t)$ denote the height of the ball at time t. The height turns out to be given by the following form (a parabola or quadratic function)

$$x(t) = \frac{1}{2}a_g t^2 + vt + h_0 \qquad (2.9)$$

where a_g, v, h_0 are constants.

The precise values of these constants determine the motion of the ball, so they have physical interpretations. In fact, the subscript on a_g indicates that it comes from gravity. Let $s(t) = x'(t)$ and using Equation 2.6, we calculate:

$$s(t) = \frac{d}{dt}x(t) = a_g t + v. \qquad (2.10)$$

The annoying factor of 1/2 in Equation 2.9 has disappeared. The function $s(t)$ has the interpretation of the instantaneous speed of the ball at time t, in the vertical direction. Therefore, at the initial time, we have

$$s(0) = \left[\frac{d}{dt}x(t)\right]_{t=0} = v. \qquad (2.11)$$

This is our physical interpretation: v is just the speed of the ball at time $t = 0$, the time it was thrown.

In a game played in Chicago on August 20, 1974, pitcher Nolan Ryan threw a fastball that was officially clocked at 100.9 mi/hr; if he had thrown it straight up, this would be an example of v. The constant h_0 is also easy to understand. It's an overall constant added to the height for all t, so it's as if the game were played in Denver (the mile-high city) instead of Chicago, which is closer to sea level. For this reason, h_0 is rather boring. In fact, we could shift it away by defining our coordinate axes to have the origin in Denver.

We have only the most interesting of the three constants, a_g, left to analyze. Since finding the instantaneous rate of change worked so well before, let's do it again. From Equation 2.10 we find immediately that

$$\frac{d}{dt}s(t) = a_g$$

Therefore, the correct physical interpretation of a_g is that it is the rate of change of velocity, otherwise known as **acceleration**. If a person tries to jump up from the surface of the Earth with initial velocity 1 meter/second (m/s), they might hope to continue flying away at 1 m/s forever. If so, they will be disappointed. Gravity will quickly set to work adjusting their velocity in favor of a return to the Earth. The velocity will drop from 1 to 0.5 to 0.2 and then to zero, at which point it will actually become negative and they will fall back to Earth. The same thing happens to Nolan Ryan's baseball, thrown straight up. Thus, the constant a_g is something that adjusts the velocity and is directly related to the strength of gravity. It is also related to the size of the Earth, since it is, after all, the Earth's gravity that pulls the baseball back.

Note that the acceleration is $\frac{d}{dt}s(t)$, but $s(t)$ is in turn the derivative of something else:

$$a_g = \frac{d}{dt}s(t) \text{ while } s(t) = \frac{d}{dt}x(t) \Rightarrow a_g = \frac{d^2}{dt^2}x(t) \qquad (2.12)$$

The notation on the right of (2.12) is not really the square of anything in the traditional sense; let's agree that d^2/dt^2 means to take the derivative, and then take the derivative again of what's left. This is called, not surprisingly, the **second derivative**. In the prime notation introduced in Equation 2.5, the second derivative would be written as $x''(t)$.

ACCELERATION DUE TO GRAVITY

The **acceleration due to gravity** is the acceleration that an object experiences because of gravity when it falls freely close to the surface of a massive body, such as a planet (also known as the acceleration of freefall). Its value can be calculated from the formula

$$a_g = \frac{GM}{(R+H)^2} \qquad (2.13)$$

where M is the mass of the gravitating body (such as the Earth), R is the radius of the body, H is the height above the surface, and

$$G = 6.6742 \times 10^{-11} \, N \, m^2 \, / \, kg^2$$

is a universal constant. Here, N denotes a unit of force, called the **newton**, named after Isaac Newton, who first gave the correct definition of force. A newton is defined to be the amount of force required to increase the speed of a 1-kilogram mass by 1 meter per second, during each second that the force is applied. Clearly, to apply such a force would require work to be done, and this is the basis for the mathematically rigorous definition of work that's in use by physicists today. We will return to these points in Chapter 3.

If the falling object is near the surface of the gravitating body, then in Equation 2.13, H is very small compared to R, and so it is a very good approximation to take $R + H \approx R$, in which case Equation 2.13 takes the simpler form

$$a_g = \frac{GM}{R^2} \qquad (2.14)$$

For a "terrestrial" experiment such as dropping a football from the top of the Empire State Building (don't try this one yourself), the approximation that a_g does not depend on H is a very good approximation. For the Earth, $a_g \approx -9.8 m/s^2$. On other planets and moons, the values of the acceleration due to gravity may be very different, resulting in different weights for the same object on these various worlds. By contrast, the value of a_g on the Earth's

Moon is $a_{g, \, moon} \approx -1.6 \; m/s^2$, or about one-sixth the value on Earth. In an experiment where G, R and a_g are measured to great accuracy, the relation $a_g = GM/R^2$ may be helpful for determining M. This method is sometimes used to calculate the mass of the Earth.

MOTION IN THREE DIMENSIONS

All of the physics we have done so far involved objects falling or being thrown straight up and then falling. These are called "one-dimensional problems" because the position of the object can be described by one number (for instance, the height). Even in that case, our one coordinate would have been ambiguous without the choice of a coordinate system. Our height function $x(t)$ measured distance along some vertical axis whose origin was located at sea level (or perhaps at the height of Nolan Ryan's arm, if we are solving for the motion of a baseball).

In the real universe, in order to specify the position of a particle, we need to choose a coordinate system and then give *three* spatial coordinates. Specifying the particle's position at all times is equivalent to specifying three functions of time, which are typically called $x(t)$, $y(t)$ and $z(t)$. When we want to denote all three of them with a single letter, we will use an arrow over the letter:

$$\vec{r}(t) = (x(t), y(t), z(t)) \qquad (2.15)$$

Given any two points O, P in three-dimensional space, one may draw the directed line segment, or arrow, from O to P. We will consider two arrows to be "the same" if they are the same length, parallel, and point in the same direction (though they may be located in different regions of space). Clearly, given the arrow from O to P, we can move it (carefully, so as not to change the direction it points or its length) until O is located at the origin (0, 0, 0).

Each point P in three-dimensional space determines an arrow; just let the arrow begin at the origin (0, 0, 0) and end at the point P. This arrow could also be uniquely described by giving

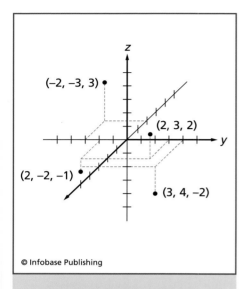

© Infobase Publishing

Figure 2.2 *Vectors in three-dimensional space.*

the angle it makes to each of the three axes, and its length. There are many descriptions of the same arrow, but the basic information is clear enough: just like a road sign, it tells you the *direction* to go (three angles with respect to the three axes) and how far (length).

Thus, an arrow can be thought of physically as a displacement, an instruction to move a certain distance in a certain direction. **Vector** is a word meaning something that conducts something else from one location to another location; thus, physical displacements are called vectors. *Figure 2.2* shows a few randomly selected three-dimensional vectors. One may specify a vector by giving the three components of a point *P*, with the unwritten understanding that the vector is to point from the origin to *P*.

What happens if we get displaced once, in a certain direction, and then get displaced a second time, in a different direction? Let $\vec{v} = (v_1, v_2, v_3)$ and $\vec{w} = (w_1, w_2, w_3)$ be vectors representing the first and second displacement. This is like moving from New York to Chicago, and then from Chicago to Dallas. There is, however, a single vector that describes the move from New York to Dallas, and it is given by the following formula:

$$\vec{v} + \vec{w} = (v_1 + w_1, v_2 + w_2, v_3 + w_3). \qquad (2.16)$$

In other words, we add the components separately. The operation described by Equation 2.16 is called **vector addition**, and vector

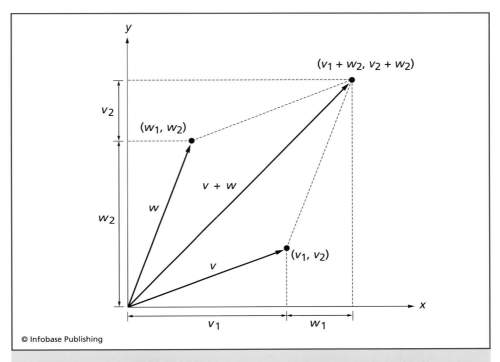

Figure 2.3 *The "parallelogram rule" for vector addition with two-dimensional vectors. The same idea works in three dimensions.*

subtraction $\vec{v} - \vec{w}$ is defined similarly. Equation 2.16 is sometimes called the parallelogram rule, because if $\vec{v}$ and $\vec{w}$ form two sides of a parallelogram, then $\vec{v} + \vec{w}$ will form the main diagonal of the same parallelogram. *Figure 2.3* illustrates the principle in two-dimensional space.

The length of $\vec{v}$ may be calculated using the Pythagorean theorem in three dimensions (which follows from the Pythagorean theorem in two dimensions, done twice), and the answer is

$$\text{Length of } \vec{v} \; = \; |\vec{v}| \; = \; \sqrt{v_1^{\,2} + v_2^{\,2} + v_3^{\,3}}$$

where $|\vec{v}|$ is just the notation for length. Vertical bars also denote absolute value; there is no conflict because if $\vec{v}$ has only one component, then $|\vec{v}|$ is the absolute value of that component.

Our entire previous discussion that led to the definition of the derivative carries over without difficulties to the situation in which $f(t)$ is replaced by $\vec{r}(t)$, the vector of three functions familiar from Equation 2.15. In particular, we are free to write down expressions such as

$$\frac{\delta \vec{r}}{\delta t} = \frac{\vec{r}(t + \delta t) - \vec{r}(t)}{\delta t}$$

where the minus on the right side is interpreted as in Equation 2.16. One might say, "But $\vec{r}(t + \delta t) - \vec{r}(t)$ is a vector; what does it mean to divide it by δt, which is a (small) number?" One would be right to question this, because we have not yet defined what it means to multiply or divide a vector by a number.

Dividing by δt is the same as multiplying by $1/\delta t$. Multiplying a vector $\vec{v}$ by a number a is defined to be the new vector whose components are

$$a\vec{v} = (av_1, av_2, av_3).$$

Equipped with the proper definition of how to multiply a vector by a number, we may return to the case of considering $\delta \vec{r}/\delta t$, in the limit as $\delta t \to 0$, analogously to our previous work for a single function. A short calculation will yield

$$\vec{r}'(t) = (x'(t), y'(t), z'(t)) \tag{2.17}$$

The arrow described by $r'(t)$ has an interesting physical interpretation. This arrow, when displaced to have its initial point at the particle position $\vec{r}(t)$, will then point in the direction the particle is going next! If you do not believe this last statement, consider a particle moving on a helix (otherwise known as a Slinky or the shape of one-half of a DNA strand), whose position vector might be

$$\vec{r}(t) = (\cos t, \sin t, t) \tag{2.18}$$

Draw the trajectory of Equation 2.18 on a piece of paper, and then move your pencil along the trajectory as if the tip of your pencil were a particle. Then calculate $\vec{r}'(t)$ from Equation 2.17 and figure out which direction the vector is pointing for 10 points equally spaced around one turn around the helix. You may need a calculator for the last part.

As a simple example, note that if a particle is moving in the x-direction, its velocity vector is just $\vec{r}'(t) = (x'(t), 0, 0)$; hence $|\vec{r}'(t)| = \sqrt{x'(t)^2} = |x'(t)|$. Thus, in this case, the length of $\vec{r}'(t)$ is the instantaneous speed, which continues to hold in general.

Since we had so much success taking the derivative of a vector, let's do it again. The rate of change of the velocity vector is

$$a(t) = \frac{d}{dt}\vec{r}'(t) = \vec{r}''(t)$$

This is called the acceleration vector. Its length $|\vec{a}(t)|$ is simply called the acceleration. We saw an example of an acceleration previously in Equation 2.14.

The mathematics of moving bodies has a lot of appeal because it can be described using elementary concepts from geometry, such as slope, arrows, and the Pythagorean theorem, and yet it has universal applicability in every branch of science, including the social sciences. This subject goes by the name of **calculus** and was originally invented by Newton (and independently by Leibniz at around the same time), who invented it in order to study the physics of our solar system, for which it is absolutely essential and the only possible way to fully understand the mechanics.

CHAPTER 3

Newton, Kepler, and Gravity

JOHANNES KEPLER WAS AN ACCOMPLISHED MATHEMATICIAN, but he is best known for writing down the first correct empirical description of planetary motion in the solar system, and in particular for noting that the planets move along ellipses with the Sun at one of the foci. Kepler's observations would not have been possible without the impressive astronomical data collected by Kepler's teacher, Tycho Brahe (*Figure 3.1*).

Tycho Brahe's contributions to astronomy were enormous. He designed and built new instruments, meticulously calibrating them and checking their accuracy periodically, which ultimately revolutionized astronomical instrumentation. While earlier astronomers had been content to observe the positions of heavenly bodies at certain points of their orbits, Brahe and his students observed these bodies throughout their orbits. As a result, Brahe was the first to notice many orbital anomalies. Without such a complete and accurate set of observations, Kepler could not have discovered his empirical laws for planetary motion.

Figure 3.1 *Kepler's work built heavily on that of Tycho Brahe (1546–1601), pictured above, who designed, built, and calibrated new instruments in order to observe the positions of planets and stars throughout their orbits.*

KEPLER'S DISCOVERIES

In undertaking the analysis of Brahe's data, Kepler distilled a few of the most salient features of the data, which can be expressed using elegant mathematical relationships. It is to be emphasized that these relationships were not derived from fundamental physics; rather, they were extrapolated from the data. For these reasons, instead of calling these features Kepler's laws, as the usual terminology would dictate, we will consider them "facts," because they are factual and true aspects of Brahe's data.

Thus, let's consider Kepler's first "fact" to be that the motion of each planet is an ellipse with the Sun (approximately) at one of the foci.

Before discussing this further, let us give the proper definition of an ellipse. Let F_1 and F_2 be any two points in a plane. Let $d(P, Q)$ denote the standard distance function between two points P and Q. An **ellipse** is the set of points P satisfying

$$d(P, F_1) + d(P, F_2) = 2a$$

where a is a constant, which is called the semi-major axis. It is one-half the major axis, as in *Figure 3.2*.

The points F_1 and F_2 are called the **foci** (plural of "focus") of the ellipse, and they are analogous to the center of a circle. Unless the ellipse is a circle, however, neither of the foci lie at the geometric center of the figure; when it is a circle, they both do.

Kepler believed that in the case of planetary orbits, one of the foci would be located at the sun's center. It was later discovered that the focus of the orbital ellipse is, in fact, located at the center of gravity of the planet-Sun system. The **center of gravity** is a weighted average of the positions of the various objects under consideration; it is weighted so that objects of higher mass contribute more heavily to the average. If the masses are very unequal, as with a planet and the Sun, the center of gravity lies close to the center of the heavy object.

Because the Sun is much heavier than Mars, the correction to Fact 1 due to the shifting of the center of gravity is too small to have been noted by Kepler. Nevertheless, the Sun also moves in response to motions of its planets, and motions of this type have become an important tool in the search for **extrasolar planets** (that is, planets in other solar systems). An Earth-sized planet orbiting a distant star would be far too dim to be seen directly with any terrestrial telescope. However, as the remote planet orbits the remote star, the star moves in a "mirror image orbit" around the common center of gravity. It is a much smaller orbit and a much slower motion,

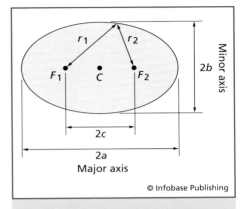

Figure 3.2 *Illustration of an ellipse with semi-major axis a, and foci F₁ and F₂.*

because the center of gravity is very close to the center of that star, but it can still be detected by precise measurements. Recently a few extrasolar planets have been found, mostly the size of Jupiter. The current status of the search for planets like Earth is described on the Planet Quest website, part of NASA's Jet Propulsion Lab.

Let's consider Kepler's second "fact," that the line joining the planet to the Sun sweeps out equal areas in equal times as the planet travels around the ellipse.

Fact 2 is most easily understood with the help of *Figure 3.3*. Note that the point of the closest approach of a planet to the Sun is called the **perihelion**, and the point where they are furthest apart is considered the aphelion. As seen in Figure 3.3, a line joining a planet and the Sun sweeps out equal areas during equal intervals of time. Therefore, the planet moves faster when nearer the Sun, or at the perihelion, and slowest when the planet is near aphelion.

Finally, Kepler's third "fact" states that the square of the period of a planet orbiting the Sun equals the cube of the semi-major axis.

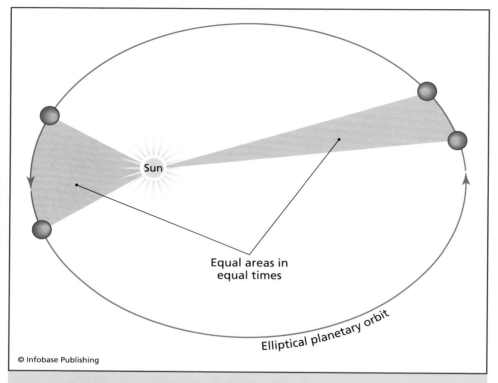

Sun

Equal areas in
equal times

Elliptical planetary orbit

© Infobase Publishing

Figure 3.3 *Illustration of Kepler's "equal areas in equal times" discovery.*

A convenient unit of measurement for periods is the Earth
year, and a convenient unit for distances is the average separation
of the Earth from the Sun, which is called an astronomical unit
(AU). If these units are used to express the quantities in Fact 3,
then the relationship has the simpler form

$$T^2 = R^3 \qquad\qquad (3.1)$$

where T is the period in years, and R is the semi-major axis in
AU; the semi-major axis reduces to the radius in case of a spherical orbit.

As an example, let's calculate the semi-major axis of the orbit of Mars from the orbital period. The time for Mars to orbit the Sun is observed to be $T = 1.88$ Earth-years. Thus, using Equation 3.1, the length of the semi-major axis for Mars' orbit is $R = T^{2/3} = 1.52$ AU.

NEWTON'S LAWS OF MOTION

Newton's laws of motion, together with Newton's law of universal gravitation and the mathematical techniques of calculus, provided for the first time a unified explanation for a wide range of physical phenomena, most of which had been studied by scientists and philosophers before Newton, who had come to various partial, incorrect, or approximate solutions. The phenomena for which Newton's theory works well include the motion of spinning bodies; motion of bodies in fluids; projectile motion; sliding along an inclined plane; motion of a pendulum; tides of the oceans; and the orbits of planets and moons. In particular, Kepler's rules for planetary motion follow from Newton's theory, as we shall see in a later section. The law of conservation of momentum, which Newton derived as a corollary of his second and third laws, was the first conservation law to be discovered.

Despite the impressive successes of Newton's theory, it's important to realize that it is very far from the whole story. In particular, it is completely incorrect as a description of atomic or subatomic physics. When applied to an atom, a Newtonian treatment of the forces involved implies that the atom should collapse and we should not be here! To explain why there are distinct atomic orbitals for electrons, and hence why the basic processes of chemistry (such as covalent and ionic bonds) occur, one needs quantum mechanics. The inception of quantum mechanics can be traced to Max Planck's treatment of blackbody radiation in 1900, which is separated from Newton's discoveries by about two centuries. We will discuss blackbody radiation in Chapter 6.

Newtonian mechanics is inadequate to describe the dynamics of galaxies, galaxy clusters, or black holes. Newton's theory also does not correctly describe the detailed properties of the electromagnetic field. A detailed theory of the electromagnetic field was developed by James Clerk Maxwell, but Maxwell's theory (which we do not have space to describe here) is not compatible with Newtonian physics if one attempts to understand experiments involving single photons, such as the photoelectric effect. Nonetheless, on length scales varying from tiny sand particles up to the size of a solar system, and for velocities small compared to the speed of light (the speed of light is $c \approx 3 \times 10^8$ meters/sec), Newtonian mechanics has proven to be an extremely good approximation. For problems near the surface of the Earth (such as modeling accelerations or collisions of cars), and for the motions of satellites, Newtonian physics is still in use today.

Newton's first law is sometimes called the law of inertia, and it states that when the net force on an object is zero, it moves in a straight line at a constant speed.

Some explanation of the term **net force** is needed here. A single force is represented by a vector

$$\vec{F} = (F_1, F_2, F_3). \tag{3.2}$$

The meaning of this is the following. Consider your intuitive notion of applying a force; for example, pushing a rock away from you. By pushing harder or softer you change the amount of force that you exert—the magnitude of the force. You could also choose a direction in which to push the rock, so the force has a direction as well. Magnitude and direction together determine a vector. When written in the component notation, as in equation (3.2), the **magnitude** is determined from the Pythagorean theorem to be

$$|\vec{F}| = \sqrt{F_1^2 + F_2^2 + F_3^2}.$$

The arrow from the point $(0, 0, 0)$ to the point (F_1, F_2, F_3) determines the direction of the force.

Vectors add via the parallelogram rule, as explained in Chapter 2. The vector sum has the physical interpretation of applying *several* forces concurrently—as if you and your friend are both pushing the rock. A more familiar example, a tug-of-war, illustrates the idea of combining forces acting along a single line, but in different directions. The condition of zero net force in Newton's first law is, in this case, equivalent to the statement that the tug-of-war is a tie—both sides are pulling, but they're equally matched and (at least for a while) the rope does not move much.

In general, the net force is the vector sum of all of the forces, which corresponds physically to the statement that all of the forces are applied to the same object at the same time. Suppose that we let $\vec{x}(t)$ denote the position vector of a particle at time t. Then the statement of the first law is

$$\vec{x}(t) = \vec{x}_0 + \vec{v}\,t \qquad (3.3)$$

where $\vec{x}_0$ and $\vec{v}$ are constant vectors representing, respectively, the position of the object at time zero, and the (constant) velocity.

Some care in the application of Equation 3.3 is advised. An object satisfying Equation 3.3 would not satisfy any similar equation in a second set of coordinates $\vec{r}(t)$, where $\vec{r}(t)$ is defined by continuously rotating $\vec{x}(t)$ about some fixed axis with some fixed angular speed. This led to the definition of an "inertial frame" to be a set of coordinates in which Newton's first law holds true.

Newton's second law is sometimes called the law of acceleration, and it states that the acceleration of an object equals the total force acting on it, divided by a constant (called the mass), which is a property of the object. The second law, in equation form, gives rise to the famous

$$\vec{F} = m\vec{a}$$

where F is force, m is mass, and a is acceleration. It is very useful to think carefully about which quantities in this equation are defined in terms of the others. In particular, most people have an intuitive notion of the meaning of the word mass, but when pressed, they often find that their intuitive notion is incomplete or incorrect.

In elementary courses, it is often emphasized that mass is a quantity that is invariant with respect to a body's location; this is as opposed to **weight**, which would be different on the Earth versus the Moon. This is because the weight of an object A is roughly speaking the magnitude of the gravitational force between that object and a much larger object P, which could be a planet. Therefore, the weight is $Gm_A m_P / r^2$, where G is the gravitational constant, m_A is the mass of A, m_P is the mass of the planet, and r is the distance between the center of the object and the center of the planet.

The above statement that mass should be invariant under change of location gives a property of mass, but we still haven't defined it. In the above expression for the weight, what is m_A? How does one calculate it, given an object? There are at least two definitions of mass in common usage, both in terms of Newton's second law. The **gravitational mass** is determined using scales and the local force of gravity; two objects at the same height above planet P are said to have the same gravitational mass if they have the same amount of attraction to planet P. The **inertial mass** is found by applying a known force to an unknown mass, measuring the acceleration, and then defining m to be F/a. Interestingly, astronauts measure inertial mass when in a "weightless" situation (meaning that they can no longer rely on the Earth's gravity to measure gravitational mass).

Newton was already well aware that the proportionality between inertia and gravitational attraction is an independent empirical fact, not something that follows from the first principles of his theory. Newton also noted that this proportionality does not apply to forces in general, citing as an example the force of magnetism, which is not proportional to the mass of the attracted body. Is the proportionality of inertial mass to gravitational mass then an accident? Whether it is or not, Einstein's general theory of relativity conceives of gravitational motion as inertial motion in curved spacetime. In such a theory, inertial mass and gravitational mass are not just accidentally proportional but they are the same concept.

One could envision a third definition of mass: if a bar of pure gold contains $N = 10^{23}$ atoms of gold, then its "atomic mass" is defined to be N times the number of protons in a single atom (79 for gold) times a constant, m_p, added to N times the number of neutrons per atom (118 for gold) times a constant, m_n, added to N times the number of electrons per nucleus (equal to the number of protons for a stable atom) times a constant, m_e. Now there are three undetermined constants: m_p, m_n and m_e. We then define the atomic mass similarly for two more stable elements and perform experiments that determine the constants m_p, m_n and m_e by setting the atomic mass equal to the gravitational-inertial mass. One may now extend the definition of atomic mass to all other elements and composite substances. Are the gravitational and inertial masses, now believed to be identical, also related to the atomic mass that we have defined here? Is there a proof of this? I will leave this as a question to be explored by the reader!

Newton's third law, sometimes called the law of reciprocal actions, states that for every force, there is a reaction force, equal in magnitude and in the opposite direction.

Consider a system of n particles, with positions $\vec{x}_1, \ldots, \vec{x}_n$. Let $\vec{F}_{ij}$ denote the force that particle i exerts on particle j. Newton's third law, given above, then states that

$$\vec{F}_{ij} = -\vec{F}_{ji}. \tag{3.4}$$

This is because multiplying all of the components of a vector by the constant -1 represents a vector of the same length, but in the opposite direction.

There is much confusion that stems from the difference between this and the so-called *strong form* of Newton's third law (thus making the above the *weak form* of the law). The weak form asserts the existence of a reciprocal force that is equal in magnitude and opposite in direction, while the strong form asserts that, additionally, the reciprocal force acts along the line joining the two particles. The strong form is satisfied by electrostatic forces and by gravity, but not by all types of forces that exist in nature. In particular, the strong form is *not* satisfied by the **Lorentz force**, which is the force exerted on a particle in the presence of a magnetic field. The Lorentz force on particle i from particle j (assuming both particles have electric charge Q) is given by

$$\vec{F}_{ij} = Q \, \vec{v}_i \times \vec{B}_j \qquad (3.5)$$

where $\vec{v}_i$ is the velocity of the ith particle and $\vec{B}_j$ is the magnetic field generated by the jth particle. In Equation 3.5, the symbol $\times$ denotes a new mathematical operation that we have not yet studied in this book: the **cross product**, also called **vector product**.

This is as good a place as any to introduce the cross product. This is a product that takes two vectors $\vec{A}$ and $\vec{B}$, and gives you back a third vector, denoted $\vec{A} \times \vec{B}$ which is guaranteed to be perpendicular to the original two. (Thus, it can't exist in two dimensions, where there are only two perpendicular directions!) Of course, given that $\vec{A} \times \vec{B}$ is perpendicular to $\vec{A}$ and $\vec{B}$ just specifies the line that it lies on, but doesn't tell us much about its direction within that line or its length. The direction is easy to describe. Assume your right hand is stretched out flat, with the thumb extended. If the index finger on your right hand points along $\vec{A}$, while $\vec{B}$ comes straight out of your palm, then $\vec{A} \times \vec{B}$ is in the direction of your thumb. The length is given by

$$|\vec{A} \times \vec{B}| = AB \sin(\theta)$$

where A and B denote the lengths of the vectors with the same name, and θ is the angle from $|\vec{A}|$ to $|\vec{B}|$.

DERIVATION OF THE GRAVITATIONAL FORCE LAW

Newton derived the gravitational force law from his three laws of motion, together with certain thought experiments and data reflecting the motion of the Moon relative to the Earth. As they are illuminating, we reproduce some of Newton's arguments, phrasing them in modern language.

The actual motion of the Moon around the Earth is quite complicated due to gravitational interactions with the Sun and other nearby planets. As a reasonable first approximation, however, the Moon's orbit is roughly circular. In uniform circular motion, the **centripetal acceleration** (centripetal acceleration is the rate of change of velocity in the direction tangent to the circle) has magnitude

$$a_c = \frac{v^2}{r}$$

where v is the speed of the Moon in its orbit, and r is the orbital radius measured from the center of the Earth to the center of the Moon. The average speed of the Moon in its orbit is

$$v = \frac{2\pi r}{T}$$

where T is the orbital period of the Moon. Thus the magnitude of the centripetal acceleration is

$$a_c = \frac{1}{r}\left(\frac{2\pi r}{T}\right)^2 = \frac{4\pi^2 r}{T^2}.$$

Both r and T may be determined from astronomical observations and long-distance surveying techniques.

The radius of the lunar orbit is about 3.84×10^8 m, and the orbital period of revolution is 27.3 days, or about 2.36×10^6 seconds. Substituting these numerical values into the preceding formula, we find

$$a_c = 2.72 \times 10^{-3} \, m/s^2.$$

Let a_e denote the acceleration due to gravity on the surface of the Earth, and let a_m denote the acceleration due to Earth's gravity at the distance of the lunar orbit. Then

The Lunar Calendar

Calendars based on the lunar orbital period of 27.3 days are still in use in most areas of the world. The Islamic calendar is the calendar used to date events in predominantly Muslim countries and used by Muslims everywhere to determine the proper day on which to celebrate Muslim holy days. It is a purely lunar calendar having 12 lunar months in a year of about 354 days. By contrast, The Chinese calendar is a lunisolar calendar formed by combining a purely lunar calendar with a solar calendar. This combination is performed by inserting an extra month every second or third year, so that the same months approximately correspond to the same seasons.

$$\frac{a_e}{a_m} = \frac{9.81 \, m/s^2}{2.72 \times 10^{-3} \, m/s^2} \approx 3600.$$

On the other hand,

$$\frac{radius(lunar \; orbit)}{radius(Earth)} = \frac{3.84 \times 10^8 \, m}{6.37 \times 10^6 \, m} \approx 60.$$

Since $60^2 = 3600$, one may conclude that the acceleration caused by the gravitational force evidently decreases proportionally to the inverse square of the distance. By the second law, F is proportional to a, so the gravitational force must also vary inversely to the square of the distance. In other words,

$$F_{grav} \propto \frac{1}{r^2}$$

where r is the distance between the Earth's center and the center of the Moon, and the symbol "$\propto$" means "proportional to."

Newton then reasoned that the strength of the gravitational interaction between the Earth and the Moon depends strongly on the masses of the two objects, and not strongly on other physical properties, such as chemical composition. It certainly didn't have to be this way. Nevertheless, Newton's intuition was correct: we live in a universe where nongravitational interactions between the Earth and the Moon are negligible, and where the strength of the interaction is governed by the mass.

Let M be the mass of the Earth and m be that of the Moon. With these assumptions and using the third law of motion, the Earth exerts a force $F_{M \, on \, m}$ on the Moon that is equal and opposite to the force $F_{m \, on \, M}$ exerted by the Moon on the Earth. More precisely, these forces are equal in magnitude but opposite in direction:

$$\vec{F}_{M \, on \, m} = -\vec{F}_{m \, on \, M}.$$

In particular, the length (or magnitude) of these two vectors is the same. Let's call their common magnitude $F(M,m)$. Then our argument shows that this is a symmetric function:

$$F(M,m) = F(m,M). \qquad (3.6)$$

The symmetry of Equation 3.6 implies that the function F is a sum of terms that take the form of a sum or product of the two masses, that is,

$$F_{grav} = A(M+m) + BMm \qquad (3.7)$$

for some constants A, B. We can in fact rule out all possibilities except the first power of the product of the masses by appealing to the second law and to experiment.

We now describe some very important experiments, originally due to Galileo, that help to fix the functional form of F. Consider the hypothetical action of dropping an object off of the top of the Empire State Building. It has been observed that if we neglect the effects of air resistance, then any object you could drop would reach the ground at the same time, *regardless of the mass of the object!* In other words, if we fix a mass M, and consider dropping other objects of masses $m_1, m_2, \ldots$ onto M, then the acceleration experienced by these objects is actually independent of $m_1, m_2, \ldots$ and so on. This has the disturbing consequence that if we dropped a chicken and a pound of lead off of a high building at the same time on a planet with no atmosphere, they would hit the ground at exactly the same time.

By the second law applied to system m, we have

$$\vec{F}_{grav} = m\vec{a}_{grav}$$

where the magnitude $|\vec{a}_{grav}|$ cannot depend on m by the above observation. Therefore, F_{grav}/m cannot depend on m, either. The only way to reconcile this with Equation 3.7 is to take $A = 0$ and $n = 1$, which implies $F_{grav} \propto Mm$, with a constant of proportionality that, as we have already seen, must depend on r and (to some good approximation) the r-dependence takes the form r^{-2}. Let's then factor out the r-dependence and call the remaining constant (which now really is constant) G, the gravitational constant. This yields the result:

$$F_{grav} = G\frac{Mm}{r^2}. \tag{3.8}$$

The constant G can be measured by experiments, and is found to have the approximate value $G \approx 6.67 \times 10^{-11}$ N m^2/kg^2. Equation 3.8 is called Newton's law of universal gravitation, though even in Newtonian mechanics, it is not a fundamental law; rather it is an analytic expression derived from the other laws and certain measurements.

The meaning of the word universal in the law of universal gravitation is questionable. The equation does seem universal in the sense that we expect it to also hold in some other part of the universe, such as the Andromeda galaxy. This property of a physical theory is called translation invariance, and it means that fundamental physics is the same here as in some other part of the universe. As intuitive as this property may sound, it is probably not correct in all cases. Some theories imply that parts of the universe might have been in contact early in the universe, but as the universe expanded they lost contact and their local laws of physics went separate ways.

Parallel universes can have different values of the fundamental constants of cosmology, such as the Newton constant, G, that we have become familiar with. It is not known whether some more fundamental theory fixes the value of G to be what it is in our universe, though we can say that had G (and other constants) been outside of a certain range, then structure such as galaxies could not have formed (and we could not exist). Imposing the condition that the universe must facilitate galaxy formation is actually a quite strong condition, and restricts one to a small corner of the space of possible values for parameters such as G. Inquiry and debate about these issues continues today; see in particular the work of Max Tegmark on parallel universes.

MACH'S PRINCIPLE

In formulating his general theory of relativity, Einstein relies on an idea that he attributes to Ernst Mach, who lived in Germany two centuries after Newton. The fundamental equations of general relativity assert that the curvature of space and time can be determined from a set of functions (the energy-momentum tensor) describing the distribution of matter and energy. This is not unrelated to Mach's statement that "mass everywhere determines inertia" statement, but it seems that Einstein molded and reformulated Mach's idea, ultimately presenting a clearer and truer version of it.

Mach states such ideas in the following sections of his book the *Science of Mechanics*, where he also objected to Newton's idea that there is an absolute space.

If, in a material spatial system, there are masses with different velocities, which can enter into mutual relations with one

another; these masses present to us forces. We can only de-
cide how great these forces are when we know the velocities
to which those masses are to be brought. Resting masses too
are forces if all the masses do not rest. . . . All masses and all
velocities, and consequently all forces, are relative. There is
no decision about relative and absolute which we can possibly
meet, to which we are forced, or from which we can obtain
any intellectual or other advantage.

This is a clear and lucid statement of the relativity of motion. Mach also proposed to define the notion of mass in terms of
acceleration and Newton's third law (action/reaction). The Web
site "From Stargazers to Starships" provides a good summary of
Mach's views on this:

When two compact objects act on each other, they accelerate
in opposite directions, and the ratio of their accelerations is
always the same.

In a sense, all three of Newton's laws follow from the preceding statement. Adopting the notion of mass definable along this
line, given two bodies A and B, Mach points out that only the *ratio*
of the masses of A and B can be defined using concepts of inertia
and acceleration. One then defines the mass of 1 liter of water
to be 1 kilogram and this, together with Mach's principle, allows
to determine all other masses. We will return to these ideas in
Chapter 6.

NEWTONIAN MECHANICS AND KEPLER'S LAWS

All three of the observations now known as Kepler's laws may be
derived from the fundamental theory put forth by Newton. As an
example, we present the derivation for the third of Kepler's observations, which relates the orbital period of a satellite to the radius
of its orbit, from the more fundamental Newtonian theory.

This supposes that the mass of the satellite is much smaller than the mass of the central body (this is more or less the definition of the term "satellite"; otherwise, it's simply a two-body system). We'll discuss satellites rotating about the Earth, but the result applies equally well to any tiny body orbiting a large one, such as the moons of Jupiter. For simplicity, we'll take the orbit to be spherical, though Kepler's observation concerned elliptical orbits as well.

Suppose that the satellite is in a circular orbit well above the Earth's atmosphere, so that we can neglect friction effects due to the viscosity of air. The mass m of the satellite is assumably constant, and the total force and the acceleration are in the same direction, towards the center of the Earth. It is also necessary to assume that m is much less than M, so that the satellite's gravitational field does not cause a measurable acceleration of the Earth.

The second law, $F = m\,\vec{a}$, when applied to the centripetal acceleration of the satellite, yields

$$\frac{GmM}{r^2} = m\frac{v^2}{r} \quad and \quad v = \frac{2\pi r}{T}$$

Solving these algebraic equations for T^2 yields

$$T^2 = \frac{4\pi^2}{GM}r^3.$$

Since by assumption $T > 0$ and $r > 0$, this equation has one real solution,

$$T = \frac{2\pi\,r^{3/2}}{\sqrt{GM}}$$

The latter equation is a more precise statement of what we called "Fact 3" above.

CHAPTER 4

Observing the Night Sky

IN CASUAL DISCOURSE, THE WORD "BRIGHTNESS" IS OFTEN used loosely. In astronomy, however, it is very useful to distinguish between **intrinsic brightness** (how much light does a star emit in a given time?) and **apparent brightness** (how much light from the star enters our pupils or strikes the mirror of our telescope?). These concepts can be illustrated by an ordinary 60-watt light bulb. You can think of the energy output of the light bulb (60 watts) as a measure of its intrinsic brightness. If you are directly below it, you shouldn't look at it for fear of damaging your eyesight. On the other hand, a single 60-watt bulb cannot suffice to illuminate a large area, such as a stadium. The light bulb's apparent brightness depends on its distance from us.

Thus, the apparent brightness of a star, or other celestial object, depends on both its intrinsic brightness and its distance; the farther away it is, the lower its apparent brightness. Intrinsic brightness is also known as **luminosity**, and is frequently denoted by the letter L. Formally, the luminosity of a star is the rate at which it emits energy in the form of electromagnetic radiation. The SI unit corresponding to energy per second is the watt, named after James Watt, the Scottish engineer who redesigned the steam engine so that it provided a dramatic increase in fuel efficiency (*Figure 4.1*).

Luminosity is a quantity that relates to the internal physics of the star, rather than its distance to us. The Sun has a luminosity of approximately $L_{sun} = 3.86 \times 10^{26}$ watts. This luminosity includes not only visible light, but all electromagnetic radiation emitted by the Sun, including radio waves, γ-rays, and so on. The Sun's luminosity varies slightly with time; the number quoted above is the time-averaged value.

Since the difference between apparent brightness and luminosity depends on the distance of the object from us, we should discuss how distance measurements are made. The most common method is called **parallax**. This refers to a very simple optical illusion of sorts. Imagine that we observe a statue, and behind the statue is a map of the world, so that the statue appears to be above Europe. If we then change our position, say by walking one meter to the left, the statue might appear to be in front of China instead. Of course, the statue has not moved relative to the background, but we have. The line along which we moved, and the two lines from our two positions to the statue form an isosceles triangle, and if we know both the angle and the distance by which we have moved, then we can calculate the lengths of the remaining two sides using Euclidean geometry. If the angle is very small, the remaining two sides will be approximately the same length, and that length represents our distance to the statue.

Stellar parallax works the same way: we view a star against the background of other stars, and we make two measurements as the Earth is on two opposite sides of the Sun. Thus the "short" side of the isosceles triangle is the Earth's orbital diameter. This method was first successfully used by Friedrich Wilhelm Bessel in 1838 when he measured the distance to the star "61 Cygni."

Figure 4.1 *James Watt (1736–1819) was an engineer and inventor from Scotland whose improvements to the steam engine led to a dramatic increase in the engine's fuel efficiency, speed, and safety. Changes in the steam engine underpinned the dramatic increases in production of the Industrial Revolution.*

James Watt

In his late teens, James Watt went to London to learn to be an instrument maker, and when he returned to Glasgow, he got a job making instruments with Glasgow University, which gave him accommodation and a workshop. In 1763, John Anderson asked him to repair an early steam engine he had acquired. This early model, known as a Newcomen engine, was very inefficient. The cylinder had to be heated when steam was admitted and then gradually cooled again to condense the steam. This wastes time and fuel. Two years later, while wandering aimlessly through a park in Glasgow called Glasgow Green, Watt hit upon the idea of condensing the steam in a separate vessel. This removed the need for heating and cooling, making the engine faster, safer, and more fuel efficient. A stone in Glasgow Green marks this spot as where the Industrial Revolution really began. In 1778, Watt presented Anderson with a micrometer he had designed and made, as a gesture of thanks. In 1755, Watt was granted a patent that prevented anybody else from making a steam engine like the one he had developed. For the next 25 years, the Boulton & Watt company had a virtual monopoly over the production of steam engines. Watt worked out how much each company that used his steam engine saved by using the engine, rather than a team of horses. The company then had to pay him one-third of this figure every year for 25 years!

FLUX AND SOLAR PANELS

The apparent brightness of a star is closely related to its flux, denoted f. The **flux** of a star is the rate per unit area at which its energy strikes a surface held perpendicular to the star's rays; flux can be measured in watts per square meter.

Consider a sphere of radius d centered on a light source of luminosity L. The flux of light energy through the sphere is the luminosity of the light source divided by the sphere's area:

$$f = \frac{L}{4\pi d^2}. \tag{4.1}$$

The observed flux of a star falls off as the inverse square of its distance. The Sun's flux at the Earth's location is

$$f_{sun} = \frac{L_{sun}}{4\pi(1\,AU)^2} = 1370\,watts/m^2.$$

More precisely, this would be the flux experienced at noon on the equator during an equinox. This flux is the same as the flux from a 100-watt light bulb viewed from a distance of 7 cm.

This calculation shows that solar power is a potentially potent power source on Earth. If it were possible to build a solar panel that could operate at 80% efficiency, then a 1-meter square panel would generate about 1000 watts of free electricity. In fact, solar cell engineers define a unit of illumination called the sun: one sun is defined as 1000 $watt/m^2$. Since a single lamp is about 75 watts, the flux of one sun incident on a 1-meter square panel would power all of the lights in a house, together with an array of smaller appliances at the same time.

Actual solar panels work at roughly 15% efficiency, and that's not even considering the difficulties of getting light to the panel. Our atmosphere is not transparent, there are frequent clouds, and it is night half the time. While these atmospheric factors will not go away, at least for Earth-based solar cells, it is possible that new advances in fundamental science could improve the efficiency of solar panels, which would be a great contribution to humanity.

Previously we computed the Sun's flux, knowing its luminosity and distance. In practice, astronomers measure a star's flux and distance, then compute its luminosity. The star Sirius, also known as alpha Canis Majoris, is the apparently brightest star in the night sky. The flux of Sirius is

$$f = 1.2 \times 10^{-7}\,watts/m^2.$$

To intercept 1370 watts of sunlight, you need a panel 1 meter on a side. By contrast, to intercept 1370 watts of light from Sirius, you would need a solar panel the size of Massachusetts. The distance to Sirius, computed by parallax, is

$$d = 2.637\,pc = 8.14 \times 10^{16}\,m$$

Thus, we can compute the luminosity of Sirius:

$$L = 4\pi d^2 f = 1.0 \times 10^{28}\,watts = 26\,L_{sun}$$

WHY IS THE NIGHT SKY DARK?

There is a centuries-old question about the sky: If there are infinitely many stars distributed (roughly) uniformly throughout an infinite space, then why is the night sky so dark? Note that if the Sun were suddenly moved away from us to twice its current distance, we would intercept one-quarter as many photons, but the Sun would subtend one-quarter of the angular area, so the intensity per unit area would be the same. Why isn't all of that light, from stars in every corner of the galaxy, reaching us now, even at night? This is called **Olbers' paradox**. Like any paradox, it only seems that there is a contradiction because one or more of the assumptions used in the argument is incorrect or naive. We now consider this famous problem in more detail.

Consider a thin spherical shell of stars with radius r and thickness δ centered on the Earth. If there are n stars per unit volume of the shell, then the total number of stars per shell is

$$N = n \times volume = n\,4\pi r^2 \delta.$$

Using Equation 4.1, the flux of radiation from the shell of stars will be

$$F(r) = \frac{L}{4\pi r^2}\,n\,4\pi r^2\,\delta = nL\delta. \tag{4.2}$$

This evidently does not depend on the radius r of the shell, but only on the thickness δ. The total flux of starlight from all the stars in the universe can be computed by adding up flux contributions from shells of all possible radii. Equation 4.2 shows that this will be given by the constant nL times an infinite sum

$$F_{total} = nL\sum_{all\ shells}(thickness\ of\ shell) = \infty. \qquad (4.3)$$

Equation 4.3 indicates that the night sky should be infinitely bright, while observations indicate to the contrary that it is rather dark. This paradox is named after the astronomer Heinrich Olbers, who wrote a paper on the subject in 1826, though the problem was mentioned by Thomas Digges as early as 1576. Since the conclusion is incorrect, one or more of the assumptions must have been wrong.

First, note that the number density n and luminosity L are not constant; more importantly, if the universe only extends to a distance r_{max} from us, then the total flux of starlight that we see in the sky will be

$$F \approx nL\,r_{max}.$$

The above also assumed that the universe is infinitely old, which is inconsistent with observation. If the universe has a finite age t_0 then the previous argument implies

$$F \approx nLct_0$$

where c is the speed of light.

Furthermore, Equation 4.1 follows from Euclidean geometry and assumes that the light source is stationary relative to the observer. Our universe is expanding, and as the universe expands, the light from distant sources will be **redshifted** to lower photon energies. (This "redshift" effect is described in Chapter 6.) The calculation that leads to Olbers' paradox is flawed all the way along.

HIPPARCHUS'S MEASUREMENTS AND THE VISUAL MAGNITUDE SCALE

The first recorded attempt to quantify stellar flux at visible wavelengths was made by the Greek astronomer Hipparchus in the second century B.C. Noting that stars differed in apparent brightness, Hipparchus divided them into six groups. The first-magnitude stars were the brightest in the heavens, which included Capella (alpha Aurigae), Sirius (alpha Canis Majoris), and Vega (alpha Lyrae). Hipparchus distributed the other stars according to their relative brightness, down to the dimmest that the naked eye could see, which were called sixth magnitude. Hipparchus's magnitude scale is also called the **visual magnitude** to differentiate it from other things that might have magnitudes, and because it really is, in some sense, a property of the human eye. This has the somewhat confusing consequence that the larger a star's visual magnitude, the dimmer the star.

Telescopes had not yet been invented, so in order to focus his attention on a certain area in the sky, Hipparchus used a thin tube. By around 1850, astronomers had a number of techniques allowing for more precise measurement of apparent magnitude. Any such measurement must be expressed using *some* system of units, and since we are free to choose the fundamental unit to be whatever we like, it was not hard to map the more precise measurements onto a scale in which stars that Hipparchus would have called "fourth magnitude" are mapped onto some region around the number 4.0, and so on. Careful measurements can now determine a star's flux to within 0.01 magnitudes.

Interestingly, the human eye does not see a star whose flux on Earth is twice that of another as being twice as bright. In other words, the human eye's response to flux is nonlinear. For example, if you show someone a 1-watt bulb, and a 100-watt bulb and ask them to select a bulb that is half way between the two in brightness, they will choose a 10-watt bulb! A 50-watt bulb appears to our senses to be much closer in brightness to a 10-watt bulb than to a 1-watt bulb.

This kind of relationship in which the flux (at a given distance) from a 1-watt bulb might be assigned a brightness of 1, that from a 10-watt bulb a brightness of 2, that from a 100-watt bulb a brightness of 3, and in general, a 10^n-watt bulb has brightness n, is known as a logarithmic relationship. In mathematics, **logarithms** are defined as functions having the property that the logarithm of a product equals the sum of the logarithms. As the human optical nerve responds this way, one is led to the conclusion that mathematics arises even in seemingly unrelated fields such as psychology.

Comparison of sophisticated measurements with Hipparchus's classification showed that a difference of 5 magnitudes represents a multiplicative factor of roughly 100 in flux. A first-magnitude star was then defined as exactly one hundred times brighter than a sixth-magnitude star. To illustrate, consider two stars with apparent magnitudes m_1 and m_2. The assertion that star 1 is five magnitudes brighter than star 2 corresponds mathematically to the statement that $m_2 - m_1 = 5$, which implies that

$$\frac{f_1}{f_2} = 100.$$

If $m_2 - m_1 = 1$ (that is, if star 1 is only one magnitude brighter than star 2), then

$$\frac{f_1}{f_2} = 100^{1/5} \approx 2.512.$$

A few stars are significantly brighter than one hundred times a sixth-magnitude star. By necessity, these stars are assigned magnitudes of less than 1 (Betelgeuse has a visual magnitude of 0.45). Comparatively brighter stars wound up with negative visual magnitudes. Sirius, the brightest star in the night sky, has a visual magnitude of −1.44. The full Moon has a magnitude of about −12.5, and the Sun is a bright −26.5. A magnitude greater than 6 means that the object is only visible through a telescope.

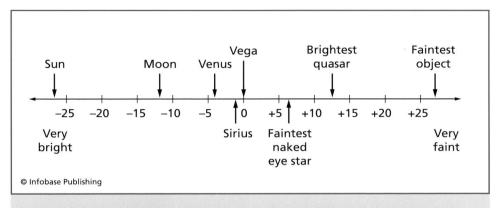

Figure 4.2 *The apparent brightness of various objects in the magnitude system.*

A 6-inch amateur telescope at a dark site can reach to 13th magnitude or so; the faintest stars in the Hubble Ultra Deep Field are about 30th magnitude. *Figure 4.2* summarizes these results.

Intrinsically, Sirius is 23 times more luminous and about twice the mass and diameter of the Sun. Of course, it's farther away from Earth than the Sun—but in fact it's very close to us, in the grand scheme of things. At a mere 8.5 light-years away, Sirius seems so bright in part because it is the fifth-closest star to the Sun.

By 1906, using a prism on a meridian transit telescope, E. Pickering at Harvard compiled a list of some 50,000 stars based on more than 1 million comparative measurements. This catalog also helped to fix the zero point for the apparent magnitude scale by reconciling the magnitude estimates from several different observers into one consistent catalog of brightnesses.

It's perfectly reasonable that two stars of different luminosities may have exactly the same magnitude (to the best precision we could ever hope to measure). The star with greater luminosity, or intrinsic brightness, simply needs to be farther away so that fewer of its photons reach us.

BLACKBODY RADIATION AND THE STEFAN-BOLTZMANN LAW

A **blackbody** is a hypothetical object that does not reflect radiation and has the property that, at each temperature, the blackbody emits the maximum amount of energy possible for that temperature. This value is known as the blackbody radiation for that temperature. True blackbodies do not exist in nature, but a very close approximation is provided by the behavior of a small hole that leads into a large box. Light entering the hole would reflect many times from the interior walls of the box and is almost certain to be absorbed in the process. Radiation that leaves the hole is emitted at every possible wavelength.

A blackbody emits a definite amount of energy at each wavelength for a particular temperature, so for each temperature, one can graph a **blackbody radiation curve**, a graph of energy versus wavelength (*Figure 4.3*). It is remarkable that these curves depend only on the temperature! The hotter the blackbody, the greater its power output per unit surface area. An incandescent light bulb (or more precisely, its filament) is an everyday example. As it gets hotter, it also gets brighter, emitting more energy from its surface in the form of photons. It may seem strange that the prototypical example of a "blackbody" would be a light bulb! Blackbodies do not reflect light, however, and therefore appear black at low temperatures, as we now explain. As is clear from the blackbody radiation curves, a blackbody radiates some nonzero amount of energy at every possible wavelength and hypothetically should always radiate some energy in the visible range of wavelengths (400 to 700 nm), so it should never appear completely black. For low temperatures, however, the energy radiated in the visible range of wavelengths may be too small to generate enough photons to register as light upon our eyes. The incandescent bulb has a high temperature, and so it generates a lot of photons at various wavelengths, including the visible range.

The **Stefan-Boltzmann law** holds that the energy radiated by a blackbody per second per unit area is proportional to the fourth

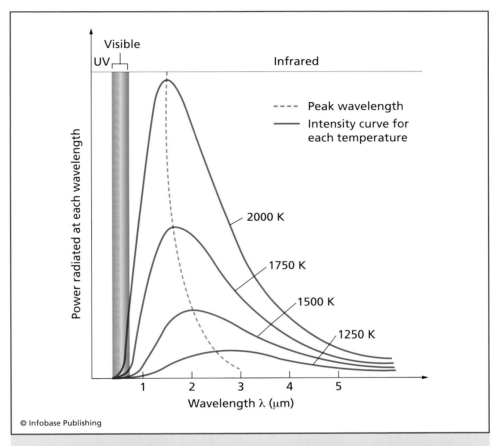

Figure 4.3 *The blackbody radiation curve is a graph of energy versus wavelength that depends only on the temperature.*

power of the temperature (with the latter measured in **Kelvins**), that is:

$$E = \sigma T^4 \tag{4.4}$$

where $\sigma \approx 5.67 \times 10^{-8}\ J/(K^4 m^2 s)$ is a constant. (Note: K, m, and s in this formula are merely units of temperature, length, and time.)

The derivation of the Stefan-Boltzmann law (Equation 4.4) is fascinating, but is also a more advanced topic than we would like to cover here. For now, note that the derivation makes use of Planck's famous formula for the power output of blackbody radiation as a function of wavelength,

$$P(\lambda) = \frac{2hc^2}{\lambda^5 (e^{hc/\lambda kT} - 1)} \qquad (4.5)$$

in which $P(\lambda)$ is the power per unit area per unit wavelength, k is Boltzmann's constant, h is Planck's constant, c is the speed of light, and T is temperature.

Planck's formula (Equation 4.5) follows from the Bose-Einstein distribution of quantum statistical mechanics. Accordingly, the Stefan-Boltzmann constant σ can be expressed in terms of more fundamental quantities: the speed of light, Boltzmann's constant, and Planck's constant. Historically, however, the discovery of Equation 4.5 led to the development of quantum theory and hence to the eventual discovery of the Bose-Einstein distribution, not the other way around. It is for this achievement that Planck is often credited with the inception of quantum mechanics, although most details of quantum theory as we know it today were developed by others.

THE HERTZSPRUNG-RUSSELL DIAGRAM AND THE MAIN SEQUENCE

After reading the last section, the reader may be tempted to speculate that, although interesting, this discussion of blackbody radiation, and the ensuing inception of quantum theory, has no place in a chapter on observing the night sky. In reality, Equations 4.4 and 4.5 are responsible for the identification of the so-called "main sequence" of visible stars, which we define shortly.

Let's assume that a star radiates according to the Stefan-Boltzmann law and see what consequences we can derive. Equation 4.4 implies that the logarithm of E should be linear in T, so let's plot temperature versus magnitude of all known stars, noting

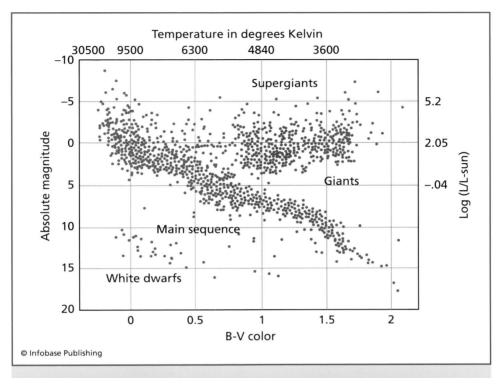

Figure 4.4 *In a Hertzsprung-Russell diagram, each star is represented by a dot, the position of each dot corresponding to the star's temperature and absolute magnitude.*

that absolute magnitude is defined on a logarithmic scale anyway, as discussed previously. Such a plot, called a **Hertzsprung-Russell diagram**, has become a standard tool of astronomers and is arguably the most famous diagram in astronomy. The standard diagram is shown in *Figure 4.4.*

The large group of stars that do (approximately) satisfy the linear relationship between the logarithm of E and the temperature are called the **main sequence**. In Figure 4.4, they can be seen as the dark line from the upper left to the lower right.

Of course, eventually, near the end of its lifetime, a star may cease to radiate as a blackbody. One speaks of the main-sequence lifetime of a star as the amount of time that it stays on the main sequence. This is related to the amount of time that it spends fusing hydrogen into helium in its core, since that fusion process allows it to be a blackbody. Since this is what stars spend most of their lives doing, the main sequence lifetime is closely related to the lifetime of the star.

CHAPTER 5

Relativity and Black Holes

The relativity theory arose from necessity, from serious and deep contradictions in the old theory from which there seemed no escape. The strength of the new theory lies in the consistency and simplicity with which it solves all these difficulties, using only a few very convincing assumptions. . . . The old mechanics is valid for small velocities and forms the limiting case of the new one. (Albert Einstein and Leopold Infeld, *The Evolution of Physics*.)

SPECIAL RELATIVITY

For a book titled *Planets, Stars, and Galaxies*, it's hard to imagine a better topic than Einstein's revolutionary discovery that space (and its identical twin, time) do not behave according to the way our intuition would expect them to behave. This intuition is built up from a lifetime of experience at velocities that are low relative to every object you can easily detect. The way that we perceive space and time is merely an aspect of our perception, but is not a good guide to discovering the fundamental physical laws. In the physical world, no velocity can ever exceed that of light, and all velocities are relative, so in fact no relative velocity can ever exceed the speed of light. This has rather dramatic consequences for a pair of observers who are traveling at nearly the speed of light relative to one another, as we shall discuss.

Most individuals are accustomed to the addition rule for velocities. If two cars approach each other from opposite directions, one going $v = 50$ km/hour and the other going $w = 45$ km/hour, then each car will perceive the other as approaching at a combined speed of $u = v + w = 50 + 45 = 95$ km/h. This is the reason that head-on collisions are the most dangerous kind! One of Einstein's many important insights was that this simple (indeed, naive) velocity addition rule holds for cars only because their velocities, relative to the Earth and to each other, are very small (compared to the velocity of light), but the same velocity addition rule does not hold for photons. In fact, at velocities near the speed of light, experimental results show that the naive velocity addition formula $u = v + w$ can be wrong by an arbitrarily large factor. Let's illustrate this with a calculation. Two spaceships approaching each other, each traveling at $v = w = 0.9c$ relative to some third observer between them, do not perceive each other as approaching at $v + w = 0.9c + 0.9c = 1.8c$; instead they each perceive the other as approaching at slightly less than 99.5% the speed of light, or $0.995c$.

In general, the law for combining velocities is given by the Einstein velocity addition formula:

$$u = \frac{v + w}{1 + vw/c^2}.$$

If c is much, much larger than v or w, then the term vw/c^2 is close to zero, and so in this limit, u is *approximately* given by $v + w$.

The work of James Clerk Maxwell and others near the end of the nineteenth century clarified the role of light (and other forms of radiation such as X-rays) as manifestations of the electromagnetic field. An oscillating magnetic field is known to create an electric field, and the changing electric field in turn creates a magnetic field. (These mechanisms can be easily checked in everyday life; any change in the magnetic environment of a coil of wire, such as moving a bar magnet closer or farther from the coil, will cause a voltage to be "induced" in the coil.) The oscillating electric/magnetic fields then can propagate along as a wave, which (assuming its frequency is in the visible range) we perceive as light. Maxwell discovered a set of equations involving the electric and magnetic fields and their derivatives, which (until one gets to the very small-length scales, such as the scale of an atom, where quantum-mechanical effects become important) form a highly accurate description of electricity, magnetism, and light.

One consequence of Maxwell's equations is that the speed of light does not depend on the velocity of the object emitting the light, although the color, frequency, energy, and momentum of the light will be shifted; when specifically applied to the frequency, this is called redshift.

The speed of light in a vacuum, denoted c, is defined to be 299,792,458 meters per second (about 186,282.4 miles per second, or 670,616,629.38 miles per hour!). Note that this speed is a definition, not a measurement; our standard of length, the meter, is defined as the distance light travels in a vacuum in 1/299,792,458 of a second). It is known that the speed of light through some sort of transparent substance, such as water, is less than the above-quoted value for c. The ratio of c to the speed of light through a medium is called the **refractive index** of the medium. Interestingly, it is this property that is responsible for the beauty of a natural rainbow!

A deeper understanding of the aforementioned properties of the speed of light and the behavior of all other speeds relative to this one fundamental speed is necessary in order to understand the structure of our universe on the very large scales considered in cosmology. We develop the basic ideas of relativity here, while a broad overview of cosmology is the subject of Chapter 6. For now, we content ourselves with the following observation: the speed of light gives an absolute "upper speed limit" on the propagation of anything else, so one may infer the finite size of the universe, assuming it has existed for a finite time.

The following illustrates how Einstein considered the problem of how to synchronize clocks at two different locations. Consider two locations A and B, and assume that they are separated by some nontrivial distance, such as the Earth-Sun distance, so light takes a measurable amount of time to travel between them. A clock at A can measure time differences for events that occur in the very immediate vicinity of A, and a clock at B can do the same for the vicinity of B. Now, we wish to synchronize the clocks, or in other words, to establish a "common time" for A and B. To do this, we assume that the time for a light signal to travel from A to B is the same as the time for a light signal to take the opposite trip from B to A. If a light-signal leaves A at time $t = 0$, is reflected off a mirror at B, and returns to A at $t = t_0$, then the time at which the signal reaches B is defined as being $t_0/2$ on both clocks. In general, both A and B could have mirrors, and the light signal could be allowed to bounce back and forth between them indefinitely. As long as the interval between one flash and the next remains constant both locations, each location infers that the other location is the same distance away as it always has been and, moreover, observers at each location can use the regular flashes to synchronize their clocks. An event happening near A is said to be simultaneous with an event happening near B if the two events happen at the same time on the synchronized clocks.

Einstein's special theory of relativity is entirely founded on two postulates. In order to state them, we need to define an **inertial frame**. First of all, a frame is equivalent to an observer; this refers to an idealization in which there is a coordinate system that covers all of space (we can take this to be x, y, z coordinates), and moreover there is a clock at each point in space and the clocks are all synchronized. In order to qualify as an inertial frame, it must be the case that the Newtonian law of motion is valid in this coordinate system. Specifically, in this coordinate system, a mass m subjected to a force F moves in accordance with the equation

$F = ma$, where a is the acceleration. Intuitively, this means that the frame is not accelerating.

The following is a useful thought experiment to illustrate the idea of an inertial frame. Imagine that you are riding on a train that has no windows and has a perfectly smooth track. Assume also that the train is moving with a perfectly constant velocity, v. You are comfortably having your lunch on the train, which includes a bowl of soup on a perfectly flat table. Under all of these assumptions, it will certainly be the case that the soup settles down evenly in the center of the bowl and the surface of the soup is in a plane parallel to the plane of the bottom of the bowl and to the plane of the table. As long as the train keeps its perfect, constant velocity, you may finish your meal in peace and in fact, *there is no experiment you can do that will allow you to determine the velocity of the train, or even whether it is moving at all*, unless you leave the train, open a window, and so on.

Now, suppose that the train begins to uniformly accelerate, that is, pick up speed with constant acceleration. Then the surface of the soup will no longer be parallel to the plane of the table. The soup will appear to "climb up the side" of the bowl as long as the acceleration continues. With this intuition in mind, let us finally state the two fundamental postulates of special relativity.

- Postulate 1: All inertial frames are equivalent with respect to all laws of physics.
- Postulate 2: The speed of light in empty space always has the same value, c.

It is a testament to Einstein's genius that an entire theory of dynamics could be based on these two statements.

In special relativity, it is very common to consider a model two-dimensional universe, with one space and one time dimension, even though we experience the physical universe at large scales as if it were comprised of three dimensions of space and one of time. It turns out that the interesting features of the space dimensions in special relativity, such as length contraction, can be trivially and immediately generalized to three dimensions once we know the answer for one dimension.

Consider two observers, each in a spaceship containing clocks and meter sticks. The space ships are moving relative to each other at a speed v close to the speed of light. Each observer will see the meter stick of the other as shorter than their own, by the same numerical factor. This factor is typically denoted by the Greek letter γ, and is given by

$$\gamma = \frac{1}{\sqrt{1 - v^2/c^2}} \geq 1$$

In our example, to each observer, the length of the other observer's meter stick will equal 1 meter divided by γ. This phenomenon has been confirmed by experimentation many times, and is known as **length contraction**.

If the one-dimensional length x is contracted by a factor $1/\gamma$, then in three dimensions, we can also define contraction by the statement that a three-dimensional displacement vector, which might be denoted by $\vec{x}$, will end up pointing in the same direction, but with its length multiplied by $1/\gamma$. In summary, to extend the concept of length contraction from one space dimension to three is very simple.

We will therefore follow convention and discuss special relativity in a world with one space dimension; this world might be affectionately be called "lineland," in analogy with Edwin A. Abbott's famous book *Flatland* (1884), which chronicled life in a world with two space dimensions. The single space coordinate is denoted x, and time is still denoted t. The coordinates (x, t) may be plotted in a plane, which is convenient for drawing on paper; such plots are typically called **space-time diagrams**. To specify the trajectory of a particle, that is, to specify its position $x(t)$ at each time t, is equivalent to drawing a smooth curve on the space-time diagram. This curve, representing the life of a single particle, is usually called the **worldline** of the particle. Straight worldlines on a space-time diagram represent uniform (that is, constant-velocity) motion (*Figure 5.1*).

The time coordinate t is the time measured on the clock of some particular observer, and x represents the position of that observer. Imagine a second observer with position x' and clock reading t'. Suppose that neither of these observers is accelerating, so that both (x, t) and (x', t') are inertial frames. Let us now use Postulates 1 and 2 to derive the equations that express x' and t' in terms of (x, t).

Postulate 1 implies that the form of the relationship must be

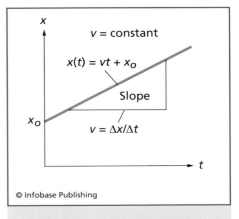

Figure 5.1 *A space-time diagram with a constant-velocity worldline.*

$$x = a x' + b t' \qquad (5.1)$$

and by symmetry

$$x' = ax - bt \qquad (5.2)$$

Newtonian physics would have predicted $x' = x - vt$, which is called the **Galilean transformation**, since Galileo also derived it, but this doesn't match the world for large v. Let S denote the observer with coordinates (x, t) and let S' denote the observer with coordinates (x', t'). The velocity of the origin in the S system as measured by S' is equal and opposite the velocity of the S' origin as measured by S. Both velocities have magnitude $v = b/a$. Now, by Postulate 2, the coordinates of a light signal in the two frames must be

$$x = ct \quad and \quad x' = ct' \qquad (5.3)$$

Substituting Equation 5.3 into Equations 5.1 and 5.2, one has

$$ct = (ac + b)t' \quad and \quad ct' = (ac - b)t.$$

Eliminating t between these last two equations and using $v = b/a$ we find

$$c^2 = a^2(c^2 - v^2).$$

Therefore,

$$a = \frac{1}{\left(1 - v^2/c^2\right)^{1/2}}.$$

This value of a is precisely what was called γ above, the length-contraction factor! Equations 5.1 and 5.2 now take the more explicit form

$$x = \gamma(x' + vt') \qquad (5.4)$$

$$x' = \gamma(x - vt). \qquad (5.5)$$

This reduces to Galileo's transformation $x' = x - vt$ when v is much smaller than c, because then γ is close to 1.

Equations 5.4 and 5.5 are called the **Lorentz transformation** equations. Using elementary algebra to turn Equations 5.4 and 5.5 around and express t, t' in terms of x, x', yields

$$t = \gamma(t' + vx'/c^2) \qquad (5.6)$$

$$t' = \gamma(t - vx/c^2). \qquad (5.7)$$

Equations 5.6 and 5.7 predict the phenomenon of time-dilation. The physics of Galileo and Newton would predict simply $t = t'$, which arises as a limiting case of (5.6) and (5.7) by taking $x \ll ct$ and $v/c \ll 1$. (The notation $A \ll B$ means "A is much less than B.")

Consider two events with coordinates (x_1, t_1) and (x_2, t_2) as seen by observer S. In special relativity (as opposed to Newtonian mechanics), we define the space-time interval between the events as

$$(\Delta s)^2 = (c\,\Delta t)^2 - (\Delta x)^2 \qquad (5.8)$$

where $\Delta t = t_2 - t_1$ and $\Delta x = x_2 - x_1$. Now consider the same two events as seen by an observer S' moving with a constant velocity v with respect to observer S. The transformation to the coordinates of S' is given by Equations 5.5 and 5.7. Thus we have

$$(\Delta x')^2 = (x_2' - x_1')^2 = \gamma^2[(x_2 - vt_2) - (x_1 - vt_1)]^2 = \gamma^2[\Delta x + v\Delta t]^2 \qquad (5.9)$$

Similarly,

$$(\Delta t')^2 = \gamma^2[(t_2 - vx_2/c^2) - (t_1 - v\,x_1/c^2)]^2 = \gamma^2[\Delta t + \frac{v}{c^2}\Delta x]^2 \qquad (5.10)$$

Now, multiply Equation 5.10 by c^2, and subtract it from Equation 5.9, expand and make all possible cancellations, to find:

$$c^2(\Delta t')^2 - (\Delta x')^2 = c^2(\Delta t)^2 - (\Delta x)^2 \qquad (5.11)$$

Equation 5.11 is striking; one should be shocked by it at first sight.

In Newtonian mechanics, the quantity $(\Delta t)^2 + (\Delta x)^2$ (which is the squared-length of the vector from one event to the other) is invariant if we make a Galilean transformation, which is necessarily of the form $x' = x - vt$, $t' = t$. In relativity (which, lest we forget, is the more correct theory), this fails and is replaced by something far more interesting. The invariant quantity that doesn't change when we go to the reference frame of a second observer, uniformly moving with respect to the first, is $c^2(\Delta t)^2 - (\Delta x)^2$, which was denoted $(\Delta s)^2$ in Equation 5.8.

The set of all points $c^2t^2 - x^2 = k$, where k is some constant, takes the form of a hyperboloid in the space-time diagram (that is, a plot with two perpendicular axes representing space and time). Lorentz transformations can be interpreted as moving us along this hyperboloid!

THE TWIN "PARADOX"

Consider a pair of twins, born on Earth. One of them boards the starship *Enterprise*, which quickly accelerates to a velocity of $0.9c$ relative to the Earth. This twin travels for what appears to him to be 10 years, then turns around and returns to Earth, where he decelerates and stops. To the traveling twin only 20 years have passed, while the prediction of relativity is that 46 years will have passed to the twin who stayed at rest on the Earth.

One might argue that we could have considered a reference frame in which the spaceship remained at rest, while the Earth moved away and came back to the spaceship. This should be an equivalent physical situation, so why isn't the twin in the spaceship the older one? This argument is incorrect. Only the Earth twin stayed in the same inertial frame. The spaceship accelerated upon leaving the Earth, at the turn-around point, and when stopping at the end, so the spaceship's frame is not inertial and hence Postulate 1 does not apply.

LENGTH OF A CURVE

We begin with the simplest version of arc length, and one that requires no calculus. The transcendental number π is defined as the ratio of the circumference of any circle to its diameter, $\pi = C/D = C/2r$, where r is the

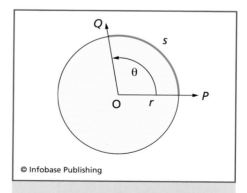

© Infobase Publishing

Figure 5.2 *In this figure, a one-radian angle is the value of θ when $s = r = 1$.*

radius. Therefore, $C = 2\pi r$. This suggests a particularly pleasant unit of angle measure (much nicer than the degree, which is completely unnatural). One **radian** of angle is defined to be the unique angle such that a wedge of that angle subtends one unit of length on a circle of radius 1 (*Figure 5.2*).

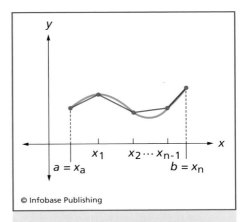

Figure 5.3 *The division of a curve into segments in order to calculate arc length.*

Now, still on the unit circle, suppose that a ray makes an angle of θ radians with the positive x-axis. Define the coordinates of the intersection of this ray with the unit circle to be $(\cos \theta, \sin \theta)$. This defines two functions from the interval $[0, 2\pi]$ into the interval $[-1, 1]$. The unit circle is then, by definition, parameterized by

$$x(t) = \cos(t),\ y(t) = \sin(t),\ t \in [0, 2\pi]. \qquad (5.12)$$

Usually, arc length for a curve in the plane is computed by (1) choosing a sequence of points lying along the curve, (2) drawing the straight line between each two successive points, (3) computing the length of each segment using the Pythagorean theorem, (4) adding up the lengths of all the segments, and, finally, (5) examining the limit as the length of each segment goes to zero simultaneously while the number of segments approaches infinity. Schematically, the division of a curve into segments is shown in *Figure 5.3*.

Each of the segments in the approximation may be viewed as the hypotenuse of a triangle. One might denote the horizontal and vertical sides of each triangle by dx and dy respectively, and the hypotenuse by ds. The Pythagorean theorem states:

$$ds^2 = dx^2 + dy^2. \qquad (5.13)$$

Adding up the contributions from all the segments and taking the limit as the number of segments goes to infinity is called "integration," and will not be treated in full detail here (see Spivak, 1980). To see that our procedure really works, however, let's use it to calculate the length of the unit circle, which we already know to be $C = 2\pi r$.

Approximate the circle by N equally spaced line segments. The jth line segment has its initial point at

$$\theta_j = \frac{2\pi(j-1)}{N} \ (radians)$$

and its final point at $2\pi \, j/N$ radians. Therefore, the Nth segment has its endpoint at 2π radians, corresponding to a full revolution around the circle. For $N = 4$, the segments form a square inscribed within the circle.

The first segment goes from the point $(1,0)$ to the point $(\cos(2\pi/N), \sin(2\pi/N))$, so the length of this (and hence every) segment is

$$Length(segment) = \sqrt{\left(1-\cos(2\pi/N)\right)^2 + \sin(2\pi/N)^2} = \sqrt{2-2\cos(2\pi/N)}.$$

Therefore, the total length of all the segments is

$$Total\ Length = \sqrt{2}N\sqrt{1-\cos(\frac{2\pi}{N})} \qquad (5.14)$$

since there are N segments. For small x, however, $1 - \cos x$ is approximately equal to $x^2/2$. Therefore,

$$Length \approx \sqrt{2}N\sqrt{\frac{1}{2}\left(\frac{2\pi}{N}\right)^2}.$$

The approximation that we used, $1 - \cos x \approx x^2/2$, gets better and better as x gets smaller. Specifically, we used it for $x = 2\pi/N$, which gets smaller as N (the number of segments) goes to infinity! So our procedure gives 2π as the limiting value for the length of the unit circle, just as we suspect.

If this seems mysterious, plug Equation 5.14 into a calculator with $N = 500$, and compare it to the numerical value for 2π, which is about 6.28.

NON-EUCLIDEAN GEOMETRY

Most geometries on the plane R^2 are non-Euclidean, but first, what is **Euclidean geometry**? Euclid's *The Elements* is one of the most famous mathematical texts of all time. Although written around 300 B.C., its content (often in a simplified form) is still taught in every middle school and high school around the world. This is truly a testament to the fact that knowledge is cumulative. What is truly remarkable about Euclid's *Elements* is the fact that the entire edifice that is now known as Euclidean geometry was built from only five postulates.

1. One may draw a straight line from any point to any other.
2. One may produce a finite straight line continuously in a straight line.
3. One may produce a circle with any center and distance.
4. All right angles are equal to each other.
5. Given a line and a point not on the line, it is possible to draw exactly one line through the given point parallel to the line.

There was much controversy over whether the fifth postulate could be derived from the other four, though now it is known to be independent. One way to prove it is independent is to construct models that satisfy the other four postulates and not the fifth. This is easily accomplished once one is willing to generalize the notion of arc length.

One could perform the same procedure used to calculate arc length in the last section, but with a different definition of *ds*, and one which contradicts the Pythagorean theorem. Clearly, if we're contradicting the Pythagorean theorem, we are moving outside of the bounds of Euclidean geometry!

The most general second degree polynomial in dx and dy that one could consider is

$$ds^2 = A(x,y)dx^2 + B(x,y)dxdy + C(x,y)dy^2. \qquad (5.15)$$

Euclidean geometry arises from Equation 5.15 through the very special choice $A = C = 1$, $B = 0$. Let us now consider a different choice, called the **Poincaré half-plane**, that arises from Equation 5.15 by setting B again to zero, and $A = C = y^{-2}$. This has the counterintuitive property that points on the x-axis (that is, with $y = 0$) cause the formula for length to give $ds = \infty$, which is not very helpful. Let's restrict the plane to $y > 0$, which means we're restricting our attention to the upper half-plane. Then, at least, Equation 5.15 with $A = C = y^2$ is well-defined for all points we're considering.

Let γ denote a path in the upper half-plane joining two points P, Q. Define the hyperbolic length of this path as follows: approximate the path with line segments as in Figure 5.3. Then, compute the hyperbolic length of each segment by dividing its ordinary length by y_1,

$$length = \frac{\sqrt{dx^2 + dy^2}}{y_1} \qquad (5.16)$$

where y_1 is the y-coordinate of the leftmost point of the segment. Do this with N segments of equal Euclidean length, let N approach infinity, and observe what value the sum of the lengths of the segments seems to be approaching. Call this value $L_H[\gamma]$, where the L is for length, and the H for hyperbolic.

Given points P, Q, consider all paths originating from P and ending at Q. It is of interest to know which path γ has the smallest value of $L_H[\gamma]$; such paths are called **geodesics**. Let's now consider whether or not Euclid's five postulates, reproduced above, hold in this new kind of geometry, assuming that we replace all occurrences of the word "line" with the word "geodesic." For many choices of the functions A, B, C in Equation 5.15, one obtains a plane geometry that will satisfy the first four of Euclid's axioms by designating the geodesics to be *lines*. By the definition of "geodesic," this automatically satisfies the postulate that any two points must have a line containing them.

Thinking of lines as geodesics, rather than as perfect straight Euclidean lines, is a very natural thing to do. After all, the shortest path along the surface of the Earth is not a straight line; it is rather like traveling along the equator, which is a circle that has the same radius as the radius of the Earth. In other words, in a general curved space, we will define the word line so that the well-worn and time-honored adage "A straight line is the shortest distance between two points" is still true!

With our generalized definition of a line, it is then straightforward to generalize all of the definitions of Euclidean geometry: a line segment is part of a line; a triangle is the region bounded by three line segments, and so on. Angles are defined as usual: When two smooth curves intersect, measure the angle between their tangent lines at the point of intersection.

For the Poincaré half-plane model, one can explicitly find all of the geodesics (whereas in many curved spaces such simple explicit solutions for the geodesics are not possible). They come in two types: vertical lines, and Euclidean-circles centered on the x-axis (though remember that the x-axis is not part of the space). *Figure 5.4* shows several of the second type of geodesic, which combine to form triangles.

It's easy to see by visual estimation that the angles in $\triangle ABC$ from Figure 5.4 do not add up to π radians (or 180°), as they would in Euclidean geometry. As it turns out, somewhat magically, the difference between π and the sum of the angles will equal the area of the triangle, where area is interpreted using the non-Euclidean metric:

$$Area(\triangle ABC) = \pi - (\angle A + \angle B + \angle C).$$

For more detail about the Poincaré half-plane, and for proofs of all these statements, see Stahl (1993) and Spivak (1980). Once you've understood integration, however, why not try to

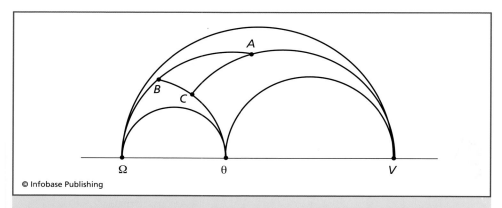

Figure 5.4 *Several geodesics in the Poincaré half-plane model of hyperbolic geometry combine to form a hyperbolic triangle.*

prove some of these properties of the Poincaré half-plane model for yourself?

THE NON-EUCLIDEAN NATURE OF OUR UNIVERSE

The previous section was not only a fun digression into a particularly simple model of a curved geometry; it also contains some of the key features of Einstein's eventual unification of gravity with special relativity, and identification of gravity as a kind of curvature. This was the celebrated **general theory of relativity**. One of the chapters in Einstein's 1920 book *Relativity: The Special and General Theory* is titled "The Space-Time Continuum of the General Theory of Relativity Is not a Euclidean Continuum." The general theory of relativity holds that space and time are inextricably linked, both parts of a single four-dimensional geometrical space, which can be (indeed, must be, in the presence of matter) curved and whose curvature gives rise to the influence we commonly know and experience as gravity.

For weak gravitational fields or empty space, the general theory of relativity reduces to the special relativity just discussed.

This is because the geometry of the four-dimensional spacetime is set up in such a way that, locally near each space-time point (or "event") there exists a coordinate system (x, t) similar to the inertial frames we have been using. Also in this local neighborhood of a space-time point, the metric or distance function, can be put into the form

$$ds^2 = c^2 \Delta t^2 - \Delta x^2$$

that we found above for the invariant relativistic interval, thus completing the statement that locally, or in situations where the gravitational field can be regarded as weak, general relativity reduces to special relativity.

Using general relativity, Einstein predicted several phenomena that were subsequently found to be accurate by experiments—phenomena that cannot be explained either using Newton's theory or by special relativity. We now describe an example of one such phenomenon. As noted in Chapter 3 (Figure 3.3), the perihelion of a planet's orbit is the unique point on its orbital trajectory when it is closest to the Sun. Let us fix our attention on a single planet, say, Mercury. If you draw a ray from the center of the Sun to Mercury's perihelion, it turns out that even in a coordinate system where the center of the Sun is fixed, the ray from the center of the Sun to the perihelion of Mercury changes ever so slightly as a function of time. The precise nature of this change is called precession; roughly speaking, this means that the tip of the ray we have drawn follows a circular path, although the length of the ray does not change. This phenomenon, called the **perihelion precession** of Mercury, was first explained properly by Einstein using general relativity.

CHAPTER 6

The Large–scale Structure of the Universe

The universe is believed to have begun about 10 billion years ago in what some have visualized as a violent explosion. The fact that galaxies are receding from us in all directions is evidence for this initial explosion and was first discovered observationally by Edwin Hubble.

EXPANSION OF THE UNIVERSE

To begin, let us introduce a commonly used unit of distance for very large scales. One **parsec** (derived from "parallax of one arc-second") is defined from the relation

$$\tan(\theta) = \frac{1\,AU}{1\,parsec}$$

where θ is an angle of one arc-second, i.e. $\theta = 1'' = 2\pi/(360° \times 60^2)$ (*Figure 6.1*).

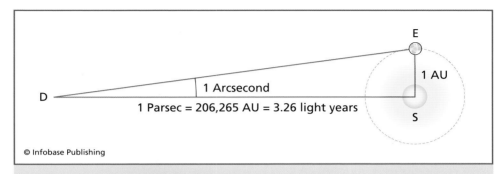

Figure 6.1 *A triangle illustrating the definition of the parsec unit.*

Table 6.1 clarifies the various measures of distance that we have encountered, and their relationships to the meter.

There is now excellent evidence for **Hubble's law**, which states that the recessional velocity v of a galaxy is proportional to its distance d from us, that is,

$$v = H_0 d$$

where H_0 is called Hubble's constant, although since it varies in time, it fails to meet the criteria for being called "constant." The reason for the terminology "constant" for H_0 is that Hubble was originally surprised that its value now should be a constant, that is, that v and d should be linearly related in this fashion (*Figures 6.2* and *6.3*). The Hubble constant frequently also appears in dimensionless form, $h = H_0 / 100$ km s^{-1} Mpc^{-1}.

The exact value of the Hubble "constant" now is still somewhat uncertain, but H_0 is generally believed to be around 70 kilometers per second for every megaparsec, so it has units of km/sec/Mpc. This means that $h \approx 0.7$ and a galaxy at a distance of 1 megaparsec from us will move away from us at a speed of about 70 km/sec, while a second galaxy 100 megaparsecs away recedes at 100 times this speed.

TABLE 6.1	Measures of Distance and Their Relationship to the Meter	
MEASURE	**RELATIONSHIP TO THE METER**
meter (m)	The fundamental unit of length in the metric system. Equal to about 3.3 feet or 1.1 yard.
kilometer (km)	Equal to 1,000 meters.
Astronomical Unit (AU)	The commonly used unit of distance in the solar system; it is equal to the average Earth-Sun distance, or 149,000,000 km.
light year (ly)	A commonly used unit of distance on galactic scales, defined to be the distance traveled by light in one year, or 9,460,000,000,000 km.
parsec (pc)	The preferred unit of distance in astronomy (outside the solar system). Defined as the distance at which 1 Astronomical Unit subtends an angle of 1 second of arc (1/3600 of a degree). Equal to 3.26 light years or 30,800,000,000,000 km.
kiloparsec (kpc)	1,000 parsecs.
megaparsec (Mpc)	1 million parsecs.

Astronomers have studied the extrapolations of galactic trajectories backwards in time. The observation was that they converge, and this would seem to imply a high-density initial state. One is tempted to say that this initial state would have been exciting to see; however, it wouldn't have been visible at all before the time of last scattering! This is something that we will explain shortly, and the time of last scattering is defined following Equation 6.2.

The **cosmological principle** states that the universe appears the same in every direction from every point in space. It amounts

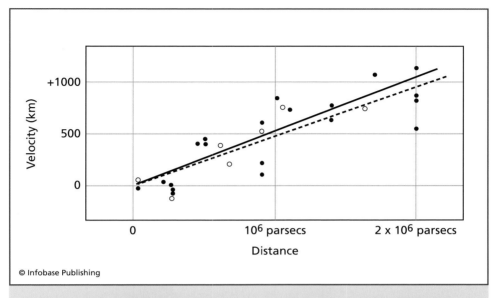

Figure 6.2 *An early Hubble diagram, illustrating the approximate linear relationship between distance (in parsecs) and recessional velocity, measured with observations of galaxies.*

to asserting that our position in the universe—when viewed on the very largest distance scales—is nothing special. One sometimes sees the word "Copernican" associated with this idea, since Copernicus was the first to carefully show that our position in the solar system is not central. Of course, Copernicus would have known nothing of galaxies, or of the large-scale structure of spacetime, but this sort of assertion is in the nature of Copernicus' defiance of the previously prevailing doctrine that we are in the center of anything.

There is considerable observational evidence for the cosmological principle, including the measured distributions of galaxies and faint radio sources, though the best evidence comes from the near-perfect uniformity of the **cosmic microwave background (CMB)** radiation, a type of energy which has its origins in the

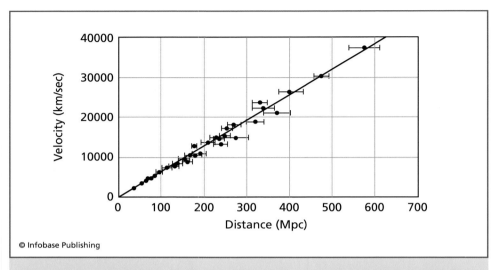

Velocity (km/sec)

Distance (Mpc)

© Infobase Publishing

Figure 6.3 *Hubble diagram based upon distances to supernovae of type 1a. Note the linearity; the slope, or Hubble constant, $H_0 = 64$ km s^{-1} Mpc^{-1}.*

early universe and yet is still passing through the Earth today and can be measured by satellites. The cosmological principle means that any observer anywhere will enjoy much the same view that we have of the large-scale structure of the universe, including the observation that the other galaxies appear to be receding.

The expansion of the universe can be difficult to visualize. One analogy that is often used is the following one. Imagine that you are a two-dimensional creature. Like a thin piece of rubber, you may bend or curve, but regardless of the curvature, you have a certain length and width, but negligible height. Now, imagine that your "universe" is the surface of a perfectly spherical balloon, which is slowly being blown up. (Real balloons are more oval, and have a "neck" where the air goes in—for the purpose of this illustration, ignore both of these features.)

As the balloon is blown up, the distance between all neighboring points grows; the two-dimensional universe expands but there is no preferred center. One may also imagine that someone has taken a marker and drawn uniformly distributed points all over the surface of the balloon. You (the two-dimensional version) are standing on one of the dots, but you can see a few of the others by means of light rays that travel geodesic paths along the curved surface to reach you. The other points that you can see appear to be receding from you.

Note that, in this analogy, you should most certainly *not* conclude that you are in the center of the universe! Remember that the surface of a sphere has no center. The interior of the sphere does, of course, have a center, but we have assumed that the universe is the boundary. Now, we are not flat creatures, so it is perhaps more useful to think of the "space" part of our universe as also being the (three-dimensional) boundary of some four-dimensional thing that is being blown up. As strange as it may sound, this is the expansion that Edwin Hubble observed!

This "balloon model" is also very consistent with general relativity. The **Friedmann-Robertson-Walker solution** of Einstein's equations with a perfect fluid matter-energy distribution (note that we are now interpreting the individual galaxies as particles in a viscous fluid!) gives a curved geometry that is well described by the balloon analogy. A simple form of this geometry has the schematic form

$$ds^2 = dt^2 - a(t)(dx^2 + dy^2 + dz^2) \tag{6.1}$$

where $a(t)$ is an increasing function of t, such as $a(t) = e^{Ht}$, and $dx^2 + dy^2 + dz^2$ represents the length in the usual flat three-dimensional geometry. Here, ds^2 is a generalization of the space-time interval that we already encountered in the case of special relativity. The time-dependent function $a(t)$ is called the **scale factor**. The definition of the Hubble parameter is $H = a'(t)/a(t)$, with H_0 defined to be its value today and $a'(t)$ is the derivative of $a(t)$.

Note that the ds^2 in Equation 6.1 has the property, consistent with special relativity, that the squared length of a relativistic interval can be negative if the space part of the interval is longer than the time part. This is fine; in practice, one almost never needs to consider the square root of this negative quantity!

The stretching of the wavelengths of photons implied by the expansion of the universe, and the associated growing of the scale factor, accounts for the redshift from distant galaxies: the wavelength of the radiation we see today is larger by the factor $a(now)/a(then)$. Astronomers denote this factor by $1 + z$, which means that an object at redshift z emitted the light seen today when the universe was smaller by a factor of $1 + z$. Normalizing the scale factor to unity today gives $a(emission) = 1/(1 + z)$.

COSMIC MICROWAVE BACKGROUND RADIATION

Light currently reaching us from the most distant known quasar (as of March 10, 2005), as may be determined from redshift measurements, was emitted at a time when the scale factor was $a = 1/(1 + z) = 0.135$. From these statements, one may conclude that the light we see from the quasar was emitted when the age of the universe was only $t_e = 0.06\, H_0^{-1} = 800$ Myr, which is about 6% of the current age of the universe. Fascinatingly, it was realized fairly recently that it is possible to look still further back into the history of the universe. The oldest photons are those belonging to the cosmic microwave background, discovered by Penzias and Wilson in 1964; collectively these photons form a snapshot of the universe at about 300,000 years, long before galaxies formed.

About 100,000 years after the Big Bang, the temperature of the universe had dropped sufficiently for electrons and protons to combine into hydrogen atoms,

$$p + e^- \rightarrow H + \gamma \qquad (6.2)$$

The symbol γ throughout this chapter denotes a gamma ray, or high-energy photon. At this time, the universe became transparent, because the photons of the cosmic microwave background radiation could no longer scatter with free electrons. This is therefore called the time of last scattering.

Following the time of last scattering, radiation was effectively unable to interact with the background gas; the radiation has propagated freely ever since, while constantly losing energy because its wavelength is stretched by the expansion of the universe. Originally, the radiation temperature was about 3000 Kelvin, whereas today it has fallen to less than 3 Kelvin! The **Cosmic Background Explorer (COBE) satellite**, launched in 1989, measured the spectrum of the cosmic microwave background over the entire sky for a wide range of wavelengths, and thus ushered in the current "golden age" of observational and theoretical cosmology.

At any point on the sky, the spectrum of the CMB is remarkably close to an ideal blackbody spectrum, as shown in *Figure 6.4.*

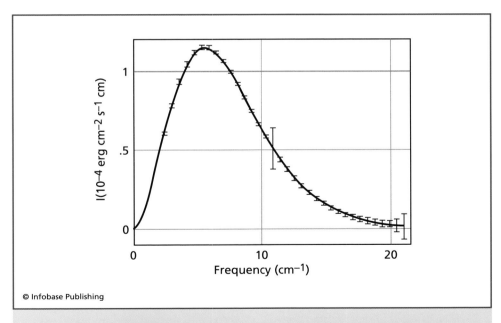

© Infobase Publishing

Figure 6.4 *Intensity versus frequency for the cosmic microwave background, shown together with an ideal blackbody curve at temperature 2.7277 K.*

This blackbody spectrum, it is widely believed, could only have come from a universe that was hot and opaque in its early stages. The expansion of the universe has the effect that the radiation cools while its thermal spectrum remains a blackbody. You can judge for yourself how closely the match of the CMB power spectrum is to a blackbody, but note that the error bars in Figure 6.4 have been increased by 400 times to make them visible!

Small temperature fluctuations in the CMB result from small density fluctuations at the time of last scattering. In more detail, a photon that happens to be in a more dense region when the universe becomes transparent will lose energy as it climbs out of the potential well generated by the excess density. It is widely believed that the low-amplitude density fluctuations that, if present at the time of last scattering, would give rise to the CMB spectrum we observe today, and they arose from quantum mechanical fluctuations in the very early universe, which were subsequently amplified through a mechanism known as **inflation**. Inflation was proposed by Alan Guth, and it holds that there was a period in the early universe during which the expansion function $a(t)$ (mentioned previously) takes the form

$$a(t) \propto e^{Ht}$$

NUCLEOSYNTHESIS OF THE LIGHT ELEMENTS

Although we can't directly observe the first 400 millennia of the universe, we can still deduce indirectly various properties of the natural world at those earlier times. For instance, we know that in the early universe, neutral hydrogen atoms couldn't exist because some of the cosmic background photons had energies larger than the hydrogen ionization energy, which is $\chi = 13.6\text{eV}$. An **electron volt** (eV) is the amount of energy gained by a single unbound electron when it falls through an electrostatic potential difference of one volt. This is a very small amount of energy by usual standards, $1.6 \times 10^{-19} J$. Just as there was a time when protons and electrons combined to form neutral hydrogen atoms (at $t \approx 400,000 \ years$), there must have been an earlier time when protons and neutrons combined to form atomic nuclei. This time is known as the era of **Big Bang nucleosynthesis**.

Consider, for simplicity, a deuterium (D) nucleus. This is the simplest of all compound nuclei; it consists of one proton and one neutron, bound together with a binding energy of $B = 2.22 MeV$. A gamma-ray photon with energy $\varepsilon > B$ can split deuterium, in

Helium Isotopes and the Early Universe

Elements in the periodic table are distinguished by the number of protons in the nucleus, since this determines the total charge of the nucleus, and hence the number of electrons in an electrically neutral version of the atom, which in turn mostly determines the chemical bonding properties of the atom. Natural helium is a mixture of two stable isotopes, helium-3 and helium-4. In natural helium, about one atom in 10 million is helium-3. The unstable isotopes helium-5, helium-6, and helium-8 have been synthesized. The alpha particles emitted from certain radioactive substances are identical to helium-4 nuclei (two protons and two neutrons).

It is reasonable to expect that there existed a time when bound atomic nuclei could not exist, because the cosmic background photons had energies larger than the nuclear binding energy, so as soon as the nuclei bound, they would break apart again. Prior to about one second after the Big Bang, matter—in the form of free neutrons and protons—was very hot and dense. As the universe expanded, the temperature fell and some of these nucleons were synthesized into the light elements: deuterium, helium-3, and helium-4.

a process known as photodissociation, and pictured in the schematic diagram

$$D + \gamma \rightarrow p + n. \qquad (6.3)$$

The Equation 6.3 can also run in the opposite direction; a proton and neutron can fuse to form a deuterium nucleus, with a gamma-ray photon carrying off the excess energy:

$$p + n \rightarrow D + \gamma. \qquad (6.4)$$

The process of deuterium synthesis (Equation 6.4) has obvious analogies to the radiative recombination of hydrogen, depicted in Equation 6.2. In each case, two particles are bound together, with a photon carrying away the extra energy. The main difference is the energies involved. The photodissociation energy of deuterium is $B = 2.22 MeV = 1.6 \times 10^5 \chi$.

Since the energy released when deuterium is formed is 160,000 times the energy released when a neutral hydrogen atom is formed, we expect the temperature at the time of nucleosynthesis to be 160,000 times larger than the temperature at the time of last scattering, when the universe became transparent:

$$T_{nuc} = \frac{B}{\chi} T_{ls} = (1.6 \times 10^5)(3000 \, K) = 5 \times 10^8 \, K.$$

In the most widely accepted current model for the early universe, the universe had temperature equal to T_{nuc} when its age was about 7 minutes. A basic prediction of Big Bang nucleosynthesis is that helium contributed 25% of the mass density in **baryons**, even before the first generation of stars started to "pollute" the universe with heavier elements. The helium mass fraction in the Sun is about $Y = 0.28$, but the Sun contains helium formed in earlier generations of stars. When we look at astronomical objects of different sorts, the minimum value found for the helium fraction is

$Y = 0.24$, which agrees more closely with the predictions of Big Bang nucleosynthesis.

FORMATION OF GALAXIES AND LARGE-SCALE STRUCTURE

The so-called hot Big Bang model (which basically includes all of the aforementioned ideas except for the inflation and quantum fluctuations of the very, very early universe) also provides a framework in which to understand the formation of galaxies (and other large-scale structures observed today) from more elementary kinds of matter. At about 10,000 years after the Big Bang, the temperature had fallen enough so that the energy density of the universe began to be dominated by massive particles, rather than the light and other radiation that previously dominated the universe's matter-energy distribution. This time is called **matter-radiation equality**, and it is really after this time that general relativity can be said to govern large-scale physics.

Interestingly, observations suggest that cosmic structures from galaxies ranging in size to the universe itself are held together by invisible matter whose presence is only inferred indirectly through its gravitational effects (the so-called dark matter). It is not known whether there is truly a new breed of matter that our experiments have failed to detect or whether our theoretical understanding of the mechanism underlying gravity is missing some crucial piece that would unify the theory with measurements.

It would be remiss not to mention that the current time, as this book is being written, is a very exciting time for particle physics and cosmology, in which precision measurements of the cosmic microwave background are providing us with much new information about the early universe! The references will direct you to more information about how to follow the research of current experts in this exciting field.

GLOSSARY

ACCELERATION A vector representing the rate of change of the velocity vector.

ACCELERATION DUE TO GRAVITY The acceleration that an object experiences because of gravity when it falls freely close to the surface of a massive body, such as a planet (also known as the acceleration of freefall).

APPARENT BRIGHTNESS Observer-dependent measure of the amount of light emitted by a distant body that reaches the observer.

AVERAGE RATE OF CHANGE The total change in a quantity, divided by the length of the time interval.

BARYONS A family of subatomic particles including the proton and the neutron (collectively called nucleons), as well as a number of unstable, heavier particles (called hyperons).

BIG BANG NUCLEOSYNTHESIS Era in the early universe when elementary particles first combined to form atomic nuclei.

BLACKBODY A hypothetical object that absorbs 100% of the radiation that is incident upon it.

BLACKBODY RADIATION CURVES The graph of energy radiated vs. wavelength, drawn for each temperature; see Figure 4.3.

CALCULUS The mathematics of moving bodies.

CENTER OF GRAVITY A weighted average of the positions of the various objects under consideration; it is weighted so that objects of higher mass contribute more heavily to the average.

CENTRIPETAL ACCELERATION The rate of change of velocity in the direction tangent to the circle.

CHAIN RULE Rule in calculus for finding the derivative of a composed function:

$$\frac{d}{dt}f(g(t)) = f'(g(t))\, g'(t).$$

COSMIC BACKGROUND EXPLORER (COBE) SATELLITE Launched in 1989, measured the spectrum of the CMB over the entire sky for a wide range of wavelengths.

COSMIC MICROWAVE BACKGROUND (CMB) The oldest photons in the universe, discovered by accident in 1964; collectively these photons form a snapshot of the universe at about 300,000 years, long before galaxies formed.

COSMOLOGICAL PRINCIPLE   The principle that the universe appears the same in every direction from every point in space.

CROSS PRODUCT   A product that takes two vectors $\vec{A}$ and $\vec{B}$, and gives back a third vector, denoted $\vec{A} \times \vec{B}$, which is guaranteed to be perpendicular to the original two.

DERIVATIVE   A mathematical tool representing the rate of change of one function relative to another.

ELECTRON VOLT (eV)   The amount of energy gained by a single unbound electron when it falls through an electrostatic potential difference of one volt.

ELLIPSE   The set of points P satisfying $d(P, F_1) + d(P, F_2) = 2a$ where a is a constant, which is called the semi-major axis.

EPICYCLE   The curve traced out by a point on a circle rolling along the outside of another circle.

EUCLIDEAN GEOMETRY   Geometry based on Euclid's five postulates.

EXTRASOLAR PLANETS   Planets in other solar systems.

FOCI   Two points symmetrically located on the major axis of an ellipse either side of the center.

FLUX   For a star, the rate per unit area at which its energy strikes a surface held perpendicular to the star's rays; measured in watts per square meter.

FRIEDMANN-ROBERTSON-WALKER SOLUTION   A four-dimensional geometry that solves Einstein's equations for general relativity with a matter-energy distribution resembling a perfect fluid.

GALILEAN TRANSFORMATION   The statement that in Newtonian physics, one may transform from a stationary coordinate system to one moving with a constant velocity v, by means of the formula $x' = x - vt$ and $t' = t$.

GENERAL THEORY OF RELATIVITY   A theory holding that space and time are inextricably linked, both parts of a single four-dimensional geometrical space, which can be (indeed, must be, in the presence of matter) curved and whose curvature gives rise to the influence we commonly know and experience as gravity.

GEODESIC The shortest path in a curved geometry; originally the shortest route between two points on the surface of the Earth.

GRAVITATIONAL MASS The mass as determined using scales and the local force of gravity; two objects at the same height above planet P are said to have the same gravitational mass if they have the same amount of attraction to planet P.

HERTZSPRUNG-RUSSELL DIAGRAM Plot of temperature versus magnitude for a large group of stars.

HUBBLE'S LAW A law stating that the recessional velocity v of a galaxy is proportional to its distance d from us.

INERTIAL MASS Found by applying a known force to an unknown mass, measuring the acceleration, and then defining m to be F/a.

INERTIAL FRAME A coordinate system $(\vec{x}, t)$ in which Newtonian physics, and $F = ma$ in particular, is valid.

INFLATION Proposed by Alan Guth, this theory holds that there was a period in the early universe during which the expansion function $a(t)$ takes the form $a(t) \propto e^{Ht}$.

INTRINSIC BRIGHTNESS A measure of the amount of light emitted by a distant body in per unit time.

KELVIN One Kelvin has the same size as a Celsius degree, but the zero-point on the Kelvin scale is absolute zero, rather than the freezing point of water at sea level.

LENGTH CONTRACTION According to Albert Einstein's special theory of relativity, this is the decrease in length experienced by people or objects traveling at a substantial fraction of the speed of light.

LOGARITHM By definition, $x = \log_a y$ if $a^x = y$. For example, $6 = \log_2 64$.

LORENTZ FORCE The force exerted on a particle in the presence of a magnetic field.

LORENTZ TRANSFORMATION A corrected version of the Galilean transformation, which holds that the true transformation law from one coordinate system to another moving at constant velocity v must be $x' = \gamma(x - vt)$ and $t' = \gamma(t - vx/c^2)$, where $\gamma = (1 - v^2/c^2)^{-1/2}$.

LUMINOSITY   See intrinsic brightness.

MAGNITUDE   The amount of relative force exerted—for example, as on an object.

MAIN SEQUENCE   The large group of stars that approximately satisfy the linear relationship between the logarithm of the energy and the temperature, predicted by the Stefan-Boltzmann law.

MATTER-RADIATION EQUALITY   The time when the energy density of the universe began to be dominated by massive particles, rather than light and other radiation.

NET FORCE   The vector sum of all of the forces, which corresponds physically to the statement that all of the forces are applied to the same object at the same time.

NEWTON   Defined to be the amount of force required to increase the speed of a 1-kilogram mass by 1 meter per second, during each second that the force is applied; named in honor of Sir Isaac Newton.

OLBERS' PARADOX   An argument that concludes that the night sky should be very bright, since there should be a star at every possible angle.

PARALLAX   The angle between two imaginary lines from two different observation points that meets at a star; used to measure its distance from the Earth.

PARSEC   Unit of measure in astronomy; one parsec (derived from "parallax of one arc-second") is defined from the relation $\tan(\theta) = \dfrac{1\,AU}{1\,parsec}$, where θ is an angle of one arc-second, i.e., $\theta = 1'' = 2\pi/(360° \times 60^2)$.

PERIHELION   In an elliptical orbit, the point at which the orbiting body is closest to the central body.

PERIHELION PRECESSION   Mercury's orbit is slightly elliptical and eccentric, with the closest point to the Sun called the perihelion. This perihelion advances around the Sun with each orbit, in relation to other stars that, for this purpose, can be viewed as fixed.

POINCARÉ HALF-PLANE   The upper half of the two-dimensional Cartesian plane (that is, points with $y > 0$).

POWER RULE   The rule in calculus for finding the derivative of a power function:

$$\frac{d}{dt}\left(t^n\right)=nt^{n-1}.$$

PRODUCT RULE   The rule in calculus for finding the derivative of a product function:

$$(f\,g)'=f'g+fg'.$$

QUOTIENT RULE   The rule in calculus for the derivative of a quotient of two functions:

$$\frac{d}{dt}\left(\frac{f}{g}\right)=\frac{f'g-f\,g'}{g^2}.$$

RADIAN   The natural unit of angle measure; one radian is defined to be the unique angle such that a wedge of that angle subtends one unit of length on a circle of radius 1.

REDSHIFT   For light from distant galaxies, the wavelength of the radiation we see today is larger by the factor $a(now)/a(then)$.

REFRACTIVE INDEX   The ratio of c to the speed of light through a medium.

RELATIVITY OF SIMULTANEITY   The part of special relativity theory asserting that the statement that two events are simultaneous (occur at the same time) cannot be made in an observer-independent way.

SCALE FACTOR   An increasing function of time, denoted $a(t)$, that describes the expansion of the universe in the commonly accepted Friedmann-Robertson-Walker model.

SECANT LINE   A line that intersects a curve in exactly two points.

SECOND DERIVATIVE   The derivative of a function that has already been differentiated once:

$$f''(x) = \frac{d}{dx} f'(x).$$

SLOPE   Defined for a line $y = mx + b$ to be the number m.

SPACE-TIME DIAGRAM   A two-dimensional graph in which one axis represents time and the other represents a spatial coordinate; ideal for plotting trajectories of particles in special relativity.

SPEED   Length (that is, magnitude) of the velocity vector.

STEFAN-BOLTZMANN LAW   A law holding that the energy radiated by a blackbody per second per unit area is proportional to the fourth power of the temperature, with the latter measured in Kelvins.

TANGENT LINE   A line that crosses a curve in exactly one point.

VECTOR   In general usage, something that conducts something else from one location to another location; in physics, displacements are called vectors.

VECTOR ADDITION   The operation of adding componentwise:

$$\vec{v} + \vec{w} = (v_1 + w_1, v_2 + w_2, v_3 + w_3).$$

VECTOR PRODUCT   See cross product.

VELOCITY   A vector representing the rate of change of the position of an object.

VISUAL MAGNITUDE   Classification of stars based on a logarithm of their apparent brightness, invented by the Greek astronomer Hipparchus in the second century B.C. and refined once better instruments were available.

WEIGHT   The magnitude of the gravitational force between the object being weighed and a much larger object P, which could be a planet.

WORLDLINE The entire trajectory of a particle in special or general relativity, shown on some sort of space-time diagram. Often, this refers to the trajectory of a particle undergoing uniform (constant-velocity) motion.

Aquilecchia, G. *Giordano Bruno*. Rome: Bibliotheca Biografica, 1971.

Archimedes. *The Works of Archimedes*, ed. by T.L. Heath. Mineola, NY: Dover, 2002.

Armitage, A. *Copernicus: The Founder of Modern Astronomy*. New York: A.S. Barnes, 1962.

Bartelmann, M., and P. Schneider. "Weak Gravitational Lensing." *Physics Reports* 340 (2001): 291–472.

Drake, S. *Galileo*. Oxford: Oxford University Press, 1980.

Dreyer, J.L.E. *A History of Astronomy from Thales to Kepler*. New York: Dover Publications, 1953.

Einstein, A. *Relativity: The Special and General Theory*. Translated by Robert W. Lawson. New York: Henry Holt, 1920. Available online at http://www.bartleby.com/173/.

Einstein, A., and L. Infeld. *The Evolution of Physics*. New York: Simon & Schuster, 1938.

Filippenko, A.V., and A.G. Riess, "Results from the High-Z Supernova Search Team." *Physics Reports* 307(1998): 31–44. Available online at http://www.arxiv.org/PS_cache/astro-ph/pdf/9807/9807008v1.pdf.

Finocchiaro, M.A. *Galileo and the Art of Reasoning: Rhetorical Foundations of Logic and Scientific Method*. New York: Springer, 1980.

Freedman, W.L., and M.S. Turner. "Measuring and Understanding the Universe." *Reviews of Modern Physics* 75 (2003): 1433.

French, A.P. *Special Relativity*. New York: W.W. Norton, 1968.

Ghez, A.M., et al. "The Acceleration of Stars Orbiting the Milky Way's Central Black Hole. *Nature* 407 (2000): 349. Available online at http://xxx.lanl.gov/abs/astro-ph/0009339.

Greene, B. *The Elegant Universe: Superstrings, Hidden Dimensions, and the Quest for the Ultimate Theory*. New York: Random House, 2000.

Guth, A.H. *The Inflationary Universe: The Quest for a New Theory of Cosmic Origins*. New York: Perseus Publishing, 1998.

Hawking, S. *On the Shoulders of Giants*. Philadelphia: Running Press, 2002.

Heath, T.L. *Aristarchus of Samos: The Ancient Copernicus*. Reprint of the 1913 original. New York: Dover Publications, 1981.

Heath, T.L. *A Manual of Greek Mathematics*. Oxford: Clarendon Press, 1931.

Kolb, E.W., and M.S. Turner. *The Early Universe*. Menlo Park, CA: Addison-Wesley, 1990.

Kristeller, P.O. *Eight Philosophers of the Italian Renaissance.* Stanford, CA: Stanford University Press, 1964.

Mach, E. *The Science of Mechanics.* Chicago: Open Court, 1942.

Machamer, P., ed., *The Cambridge Companion to Galileo.* Cambridge: Cambridge University Press, 1998.

Meitner, L. "Looking Back." *Bulletin of the Atomic Scientists* 20 (1964): 5.

Morgan, F. *Calculus Lite,* 3rd ed. Wellesley, MA: A.K. Peters, 2001.

Neugebauer, O. *A History of Ancient Mathematical Astronomy,* 3 Vols. New York: Springer-Verlag, 1975.

Redondi, P. *Galileo: Heretic.* Princeton, NJ: Princeton University Press, 1987.

Schutz, B.F. *A First Course In General Relativity.* Cambridge, Cambridge University Press, 1985.

Singer, D.W. *Giordano Bruno: His Life and Thought.* New York: Henry Schuman, 1950.

Spivak, M. *Calculus.* Berkeley, CA: Publish or Perish, 1980.

Stahl, S. *The Poincaré Half-Plane: A Gateway to Modern Geometry.* Sudbury, MA: Jones and Bartlett, 1993.

Swerdlow, N.M., and O. Neugebauer. *Mathematical Astronomy in Copernicus's 'De revolutionibus.'* Studies in the History of Mathematics and Physical Sciences. New York: Springer, 1984.

Tegmark, M. "Parallel Universes." *Scientific American* (May 2003): 5, 40–51.

Thorne, K.S., C.W. Misner, and J.A. Wheeler. *Gravitation.* New York: W.H. Freeman, 1973.

Tipler, P.A., and G.P. Mosca. *Physics for Scientists and Engineers: Extended Version.* New York: Palgrave Macmillan, 2003.

Weinberg, S. *Gravitation and Cosmology.* New York: John Wiley, 1972.

FURTHER READING

Web Sites

The Galileo Project
http://galileo.rice.edu/galileo.html

From Stargazers to Starships
http://www-spof.gsfc.nasa.gov/stargaze/

PICTURE CREDITS

ABOUT THE AUTHOR

GORDON RITTER   is completing his Ph.D. in the Department of Physics at Harvard University, in Cambridge, Massachusetts. He has broad research interests that span several fields of mathematics and mathematical physics, including quantum field theory and string theory, representation theory, differential geometry, quantum computation, and quantum information theory. He is also an instructor with the Boston Math Circle and has won numerous awards for outstanding teaching, including the Harvard University Certificate of Distinction in Teaching.

ABOUT THE EDITOR

DAVID G. HAASE   is Professor of Physics and Director of The Science House at North Carolina State University. He earned a B.A. in physics and mathematics at Rice University and an M.A. and Ph.D. in physics at Duke University, where he was a J.B. Duke Fellow, and has been an active researcher in experimental low temperature and nuclear physics. Dr. Haase is the founding Director of The Science House (www.science-house.org), which annually serves more than 3,000 teachers and 20,000 students across North Carolina. He has co-authored more than 120 papers in experimental physics and in science education, and has co-edited one book of student learning activities and five volumes of Conference Proceedings on K-12 Outreach from University Science Departments. Dr. Haase has received the Distinguished Service Award of the North Carolina Science Teachers Association and was chosen 1990 Professor of the Year in the State of North Carolina by the Council for the Advancement and Support of Education (CASE).